Lightning from the East

Lightning from the East
Liturgical Elements for Reformed Worship

—YEAR A—

Timothy Matthew Slemmons

CASCADE Books • Eugene, Oregon

LIGHTNING FROM THE EAST
Liturgical Elements for Reformed Worship, Year A

Copyright © 2014 Timothy Matthew Slemmons. All rights reserved. Except for brief quotations in critical publications or reviews, no part of this book may be reproduced in any manner without prior written permission from the publisher. Write: Permissions, Wipf and Stock Publishers, 199 W. 8th Ave., Suite 3, Eugene, OR 97401.

Cascade Books
An Imprint of Wipf and Stock Publishers
199 W. 8th Ave., Suite 3
Eugene, OR 97401

www.wipfandstock.com

ISBN 13: 978-1-62032-000-6

Cataloging-in-Publication data:

Slemmons, Timothy Matthew.

    Lightning from the east : liturgical elements for reformed worship, year a / Timothy Matthew Slemmons.

    xxviii + 252 p. ; 23 cm. Includes index.

    ISBN 13: 978-1-62032-000-6

    1. 1. Common lectionary (1992)—Handbooks, manuals, etc. 2. Lectionaries—Handbooks, manuals, etc. 3. Reformed Church—Liturgy—Handbooks, manuals, etc. I. Title.

BX9427 .S57 2014

Manufactured in the U.S.A.

New Revised Standard Version Bible, copyright 1989, Division of Christian Education of the National Council of the Churches of Christ in the United States of America. Used by permission. All rights reserved.

*Dedicated to the glory of God,
and in honor of my beloved sisters and brother:*

J. Claire Forster
Jennifer Slemmons Kuner
Robert Herrick Slemmons

*"How very good and pleasant it is
when kindred live together in unity!"*

Psalm 133:1

"For as the lightning comes from the east and flashes as far as the west, so will be the coming of the Son of Man."

Matthew 24:27

Contents

Series Foreword | *xi*
Preface | *xix*
Acknowledgments | *xxv*

Part I: The Christmas Cycle: *Advent—Christmas—Epiphany*

First Sunday of Advent | 3
Second Sunday of Advent | 7
Third Sunday of Advent | 10
Fourth Sunday of Advent | 13

Christmas, First Proper [ABC] (*Christmas Eve*) | 16
Christmas, Second Proper [ABC] (*Christmas Morning*) | 19
Christmas, Third Proper [ABC] (*Christmas Day*) | 23
First Sunday after Christmas | 27
Second Sunday after Christmas [ABC] | 31

Epiphany [ABC] | 34
First Sunday after Epiphany—Ordinary Time 1 (*Baptism of the Lord*) | 37
Second Sunday after Epiphany—Ordinary Time 2 | 40
Third Sunday after Epiphany—Ordinary Time 3 | 43
Fourth Sunday after Epiphany—Ordinary Time 4 | 46
Fifth Sunday after Epiphany—Ordinary Time 5 | 49
Sixth Sunday after Epiphany / Proper 1—Ordinary Time 6 | 53
Seventh Sunday after Epiphany / Proper 2—Ordinary Time 7 | 57
Eighth Sunday after Epiphany / Proper 3—Ordinary Time 8 | 61
Last Sunday after Epiphany (*Transfiguration Sunday*) | 65

Part II: The Paschal Cycle: *Lent—Easter—Pentecost*

Ash Wednesday [ABC] | 71
First Sunday in Lent | 76
Second Sunday in Lent | 79
Third Sunday in Lent | 82
Fourth Sunday in Lent | 85
Fifth Sunday in Lent | 88
Sixth Sunday in Lent (*Palm Sunday*) | 92
Sixth Sunday in Lent (*Passion Sunday*) | 96
Monday of Holy Week [ABC] | 100
Tuesday of Holy Week [ABC] | 104
Wednesday of Holy Week [ABC] | 108
Maundy Thursday [ABC] | 111
Good Friday [ABC] | 114
Easter (*The Resurrection of the Lord*) | 118
Easter Evening [ABC] | 121
Second Sunday of Easter | 124
Third Sunday of Easter | 128
Fourth Sunday of Easter | 131
Fifth Sunday of Easter | 134
Sixth Sunday of Easter | 137
Ascension of the Lord [ABC] | 141
Seventh Sunday of Easter | 144
Pentecost | 147

Part III: Ordinary Time (Proper 4–29): *Trinity—All Saints'—Christ the King*

Trinity Sunday | 153
Proper 4—Ordinary Time 9 / May 29–June 4 (*if after Trinity*) | 156
Proper 5—Ordinary Time 10 / June 5–11 (*if after Trinity*) | 159
Proper 6—Ordinary Time 11 / June 12–18 (*if after Trinity*) | 162
Proper 7—Ordinary Time 12 / June 19–25 (*if after Trinity*) | 166
Proper 8—Ordinary Time 13 / June 26–July 2 | 169

Proper 9—Ordinary Time 14 / July 3–9 | 172

Proper 10—Ordinary Time 15 / July 10–16 | 176

Proper 11—Ordinary Time 16 / July 17–23 | 179

Proper 12—Ordinary Time 17 / July 24–30 | 182

Proper 13—Ordinary Time 18 / July 31–August 6 | 186

Proper 14—Ordinary Time 19 / August 7–13 | 189

Proper 15—Ordinary Time 20 / August 14–20 | 192

Proper 16—Ordinary Time 21 / August 21–27 | 195

Proper 17—Ordinary Time 22 / August 28–September 3 | 198

Proper 18—Ordinary Time 23 / September 4–10 | 201

Proper 19—Ordinary Time 24 / September 11–17 | 204

Proper 20—Ordinary Time 25 / September 18–24 | 207

Proper 21—Ordinary Time 26 / September 25–October 1 | 210

Proper 22—Ordinary Time 27 / October 2–8 | 213

Proper 23—Ordinary Time 28 / October 9–15 | 216

Proper 24—Ordinary Time 29 / October 16–22 | 219

Proper 25—Ordinary Time 30 / October 23–29 | 222

Proper 26—Ordinary Time 31 / October 30–November 5 | 225

All Saints' Day / November 1 (or *First Sunday in November*) | 228

Proper 27—Ordinary Time 32 / November 6–12 | 231

Proper 28—Ordinary Time 33 / November 13–19 | 234

Proper 29—Ordinary Time 34 / November 20–26
(*Christ the King* or *Reign of Christ*) | 237

Index of Scripture Readings | 241

Series Foreword

THIS SERIES OF *LITURGICAL ELEMENTS FOR REFORMED WORSHIP* HAS developed over the course of more than fifteen years of ministry in Presbyterian contexts, primarily pastoral but also academic. Although this development has coincided with my own vocational (theological, homiletical, liturgical, and pastoral) formation and will therefore reflect a number of vocal variations (so to speak) that correspond to different stages of this formation, the primary concern that gave rise to this project in the first place has not diminished in the least, but has taken on an even deeper and more persistent sense of gravity and conviction. What began as a practical search for a greater variety of prayers of confession and assurances than I found in the *Book of Common Worship* (1993)—and more specifically, for prayers that reflected more directly how the Church should confess in response to specific texts found in the *Revised Common Lectionary* (1992) from week to week—has become an overriding concern that informs both my work in advocating an expansion of the lectionary, as well as my labors in the area of Reformed homiletics and worship, namely, that ongoing and continual repentance from sin in all its forms is essential, not accidental, to the Christian life, to the Reformed tradition of worship, and to the vitality and viability of the Church.

Reared as so many other pastors and seminary students have been on the textbooks of the late liturgical scholar James F. White, an ecumenically minded Methodist who served on the faculty at Notre Dame, I too quickly and uncritically adopted White's dim characterization of Reformed worship that he repeatedly describes (at least in the hands of the Swiss Reformers and their Calvinist and Puritan descendants) as "heavily penitential." This negative caricature is reinforced so often by White[1] and in the literature developed in his wake that his more posi-

---

1. James F. White, *Introduction to Christian Worship*, 3rd ed. (Nashville: Abingdon, 2000) 124, 160, 161, 189, 254, 256, et al., and *A Brief History of Christian Worship*

tive assessment of the joy with which the same tradition sang the Psalms seems jarringly inconsistent, that is, as though the connection between repentance and the joyful freedom to be discovered therein is entirely incongruous. Equally symptomatic of White's failure to appreciate the Reformed tradition is his suggestion that Calvin simply followed the Fourth Lateran Council in requiring confession before communion, as though the premier theologian of the sixteenth century applied the scriptural regulative principle to every question but this one.

White was not alone in his superficial (i.e., dour) understanding of the Reformed tradition, of course, but his conviction that "the study of Christian worship is the best way to learn ecumenism" has been influential and probably explains why many Reformed liturgical scholars today seem more eager to shun whatever may be described as "heavily penitential" than to lay claim to the true character of the Reformed tradition as *essentially* penitential, and not merely in a manner that belongs to the medieval period, from which, the ecumenist White suggests, the Reformers were not sufficiently critical to separate themselves. On the contrary, the point that should appear obvious to those who apply the principle of canonical comprehensiveness[2] in their study of Scripture and the regulative principle to their study of the Reformation is that the Reformers, in their own exegetical labors, discerned the summons to repentance resounding throughout the canon and (despite important differences in grammatical moods) on both sides of the crucifixion, resurrection, and ascension of Jesus, and they felt sufficiently convinced and convicted by it that they sought to give it a central and essential, not an auxiliary role, in their liturgical reforms. As I have said elsewhere, this essential role of repentance is signaled at least symbolically, and perhaps definitively, in the fact that the first of Luther's ninety-five theses (1517), the initial downbeat of the Reformation itself, declares that the Christian life is one of ongoing repentance. Meanwhile, the liturgical renewal movement, driven in part by the desire to avoid medieval stereotypes, has succeeded in depriving the Reformed worship tradition of one of its greatest, most distinctive, and powerful gifts: the disciplines of self-examination and robust confession that are the hallmark of true repentance and deep "reform." The services of preparation and self-examination (that last appeared in the

---

(Nashville: Abingdon, 1993) 76, 105, et al.

2. See Timothy Matthew Slemmons, *Year D: A Quadrennial Supplement to the Revised Common Lectionary* (Eugene, OR: Cascade, 2012).

1946 edition of the *Book of Common Worship*) have given way before the drive toward more frequent communion, and one can only wonder at what point, if ever, the trend toward less preparation and more "celebration" will bring to mind the long forgotten and much abused dialectic of the holy and the common.

It is from this point of deep conviction that this series of liturgical resources is sent forth, not because every element will necessarily do justice to the sense in which perpetual repentance is the most frequently overlooked and distinctive "essential tenet" of the Reformed tradition (and because the most distinctive, therefore the most essential, so to speak), but for the simple fact that repentance, self-examination, confession, and the good news of forgiveness deserve far better than to be reduced to the formulaic. It may well be that those who worship in the Reformed tradition, at least those who are unembarrassed by the essentially penitential—and undeniably joyful—character of the tradition, are best positioned to lay claim to that truth and offer it to the broader Church. On the other hand, anyone who would persist in such embarrassment, I would suggest, is not paying sufficient attention—to Scripture, to the state of the Church, to the state of the world, or the state of their own souls.

This is not to say that these elements come from on high, by any stretch, except insofar as they are a response to, and sometimes a direct voicing of, Scripture. Rather, these prayers come from the pen of one who needs to pray them. They were in no instance designed to be prescriptive, but are the best response this pastor has been able to muster as one who finds himself staring down the business end of the sword of the Word (Eph 6:17; Heb 4:12; Rev 2:12; 19:15, 21). But what a startling thing it was the first time I heard a congregation praying in unison a Prayer of Confession I had written and printed in the bulletin! Having shifted my focus entirely from the task of getting the bulletin together on Thursday afternoon to entering into worship itself on Sunday morning, I was halfway through the prayer myself before I realized: "These words sound familiar." Then it dawned on me: "Oh, yes. I wrote them."

There was nothing especially gratifying about this experience, for I have never harbored any great aspiration to put words in other people's mouths. But from that moment the prospect of writing prayers that the people of God themselves would speak in worship became a particularly sobering and serious responsibility. For, in fact, there is an inescapable sense in which "finding words for worship"[3] does in effect put words in the mouths of those in attendance: individuals of innumerable dispositions, including some who may well resist assenting (saying "Amen") to them, and churches (local, denominational, and global) whose spiritual and moral conditions need to be truthfully and honestly confessed in the presence of "God and everybody." It is no exaggeration whatsoever, but theologically and anthropologically accurate, to say that the Prayer of Confession can, by its very nature as an expression and an act of repentance, "make one's flesh crawl," for repentance is a gift from God (Acts 5:31; 11:18), but "the mind that is set on the flesh is hostile to God; it does not submit to God's law—indeed it cannot . . ." (Rom 8:6–7). Prayers of Confession then must walk a fine line, balancing "brutal" honesty with tender mercy; they must break the horse, not make it bolt.

The responsibility for liturgy is incalculably heightened when one considers that such prompting of the people is no mere stage direction; yet, per Kierkegaard's *contra*-theatrical analogy, the minister or preacher *is* a prompter whose labor is done with the expectation that the people will in fact direct the prompted words *to* God. And as if *this* were not enough, the pastor and liturgist must remember that the liturgy at points entails speaking *for* God to the people—as in the Declaration of Forgiveness, which bears the liberating function of Gospel every bit as much as does the preaching of the Word. *God* calls the people to worship. *The risen Jesus Christ* heralds the good news of forgiveness. Worship is less a work of the people (who are but the minor partners in the conversation) and more a work of *the Holy Spirit*. Yet *the Holy Trinity* condescends to enlist human agents in doing all of this work (externally speaking), much of it through the pastor as liturgist. Sobering thoughts indeed.

But such a responsibility cannot be fulfilled by a formulaic approach. The routinization of worship is deadly, even if it results from the most faithful allegiance to orthodoxy. As one pastoral colleague put the problem when I entered into this project some fifteen years ago, "So how many ways can you say, 'You are forgiven!'?" That is certainly one way of posing the question. How should one answer? To begin with: more than three.[4] On the one hand, the words of Scripture themselves are the sole written authority and norm for all elements of worship, including the Declaration

---

3. See Ruth Duck, *Finding Words for Worship: A Guide for Leaders* (Louisville: Westminster John Knox, 1995).

4. *Book of Common Worship* (Louisville: Westminster John Knox, 1993) 56–57.

of Forgiveness. On the other hand, the same Spirit who speaks through the Scriptures resists distillation of the singular gospel to a single formula, but inspires ongoing interpretation, reiteration, amplification, and elaboration as required by a wide variety of human conditions; for sin, depravity, guilt, pride, and all manner of things that exalt themselves in opposition to the Word (2 Cor 10:4) may succeed against incantation, but they will not succeed against the Church at worship recapitulating the *missio Dei* in fresh, biblically faithful ways. The Word of the LORD will not return empty (Isa 55), and the gates of hell will not prevail against the Church (Matt 16) *at worship*. As J.-J. von Allmen observed (specifically with reference to 1 Cor 11–14), the term *ecclesia* first and foremost applies to the liturgical assembly; it is not primarily a sociological term.[5] This insight, clear as it is in Scripture, has yet to sink in to the mind of the mainline churches, which seem entirely bent on sociological reform. But if von Allmen was right, and I think he was, then I would contend that the diversity of the Church need not be forced to satisfy our sociological presuppositions, whether liberal or conservative, but allowed to arise in and emerge from worship itself as the Church encounters the risen Christ and the Holy Spirit speaking through the Scriptures.

Further, if we follow this understanding of an essentially liturgical ecclesiology, and an essentially repentant orientation to the Christian life, through to their logical conclusion and point of convergence, we must finally recognize the fact that, in the temporal sphere (and whether we like it or not), Christian worship cannot be fully grasped apart from the theater of spiritual warfare by which it is surrounded and from which it is protected and held *in God* as a sanctuary—a holy "safe" zone, so to speak—an assembly around font, pulpit, and table, with the whole creation (Rom 8:19), even a host of impotent enemies (Ps 23:5), looking on.

"Safe," of course, is a relative term and begs definition in relation to its distinct referents. I would not be so naïve in this day and age to suggest that physical harm cannot come to God's people in worship, but I shall say with the psalmist, "I trust in God; I am not afraid; what can flesh do to me?" (Ps 56:4) Neither would I suggest that the holy presence of God is unambiguously "safe," so as to lose sight of the "fear of the LORD" that is due him (Ps 90:11). Nevertheless, when worship is framed in this way, the Church stands to gain a much clearer sense of what is at stake, and to

---

5. J.-J. von Allmen, *Worship: Its Theology and Practice* (New York: Oxford University Press, 1965) 43.

see people of every spiritual condition avail themselves of the healing and salvific presence of the Lord, even as worship itself serves (esthetically) as creation's libretto in the theatre of God's glory, the theatre in which "the battle is the LORD's" and the Church's vocation is to remember and give thanks for victories past and promised. As von Allmen held:

> in its liturgy the Church acts on behalf of the world, which is totally incapable of adoring and glorifying the true God, and . . . the Church [at worship] represents the world before God and protects it.[6]

In other words, the Church, as a royal priesthood in Christ, has an intercessory role to play whereby its worship, as it were, actually "protects" the world. That alone should be both good news to the whole Church and good news to the world! Hence, liturgy is really not "common worship" in any sense. On the contrary, liturgy is the divine and priestly service of the body of Christ, the service of worship performed by the Church—as it is empowered, guided, and inspired by the Holy Spirit—for God and in response to God's gracious self-revelation in the Servant Lord Jesus Christ. True liturgy unfolds under the headship, under the most excellent ministry (liturgy), and in the name of Jesus Christ, the Son of God, in whom all believers together are to serve in a united yet diversely gifted priesthood, to the eternal glory of God—and (temporarily) on behalf of a liturgically incompetent and often hostile world.

These convictions, as mentioned above, have come very slowly.[7] While I hope in future to be able to articulate these concerns and convictions more clearly and thoroughly (and defend them, if necessary), for now I must admit the evidence of this unlovely developmental plodding may be all too obvious in the liturgical elements provided here and in the three companion volumes that are planned. For this project has developed contemporaneously with my own continuing theological education and vocation, and in the weekly attempt to prepare faithful worship amidst the numerous competing demands of life and ministry; thus, all stages of this development will be represented here. This will account for the varying degrees of tone: from solemnity to exuberance, from the poetic to the prosaic, from an initial concern for avoiding overuse of masculine

---

6. Ibid., 16.

7. As I say frequently and with no irony intended, I loosely translate the Latin on my own PhD (*philosophiae doctor*) degree to read, "slow learner."

metaphors for God to a more intentional use of the biblical names of God, including Lord and Lord, etc., and a desire to avoid the far greater sin of effectively depersonalizing God by the avoidance of personal pronouns. (Where the use of Lord is concerned, my intention has been to retain this reference to the tetragrammaton, YHWH, as it is rendered in most translations of the Old Testament, and thereby direct the reader's attention to the holy name as it is used in the texts that inspired the element in question; likewise, the use of Lord is meant to reflect usage in the New Testament, which most often occurs in reference to Jesus.) In light of this peculiarly developmental quality, then, the reader may find it more helpful to approach these volumes as more of an indicative historical record, as useful artifacts, than as prescriptive in any heavy-handed or "heavily penitential" sense. They are perhaps a tidy presentation of the otherwise untidy relics of many services, a peek into one pastor's file drawers stuffed with bulletins and prayers prepared for congregations perhaps very different from the reader's own. Many, if not most, of these elements, if they are to be of service to the ongoing life of the Church at worship, will invite adaptation, in which case I simply ask that those who thus adapt them will acknowledge doing so, yet remember with kindness and favor the congregations, both the saints and their pastor, whence and among whom—by the grace of the Word and the Spirit—they first arose.

Timothy Matthew Slemmons
University of Dubuque Theological Seminary
The Feast of Epiphany, A.D. 2012

Preface

"... AND THE FIRST WILL BE LAST" (MATT 20:16). AS IT IS IN SO MANY things, so it is with the issuance of the first (sequential) volume in this series of *Liturgical Elements for Reformed Worship (LERW)*. Based on the texts for Year A of the *Revised Common Lectionary*, the present volume figures first (despite its being the last to come to fruition), although this is more accidental and circumstantial than by design. Furthermore, unless and until the prospect of lectionary expansion proposed in *Year D: A Quadrennial Supplement* and supported in *Greater Attention* takes root and grows beyond its present stage of development and swells to include further auxiliary forms, this series shall (for the forseeable future) remain at four volumes.

Among the elements included here are both my earliest attempts at writing liturgy based on the lectionary (beginning with Proper 15) and the most recent (Second Sunday of Easter), a few so recent that I have yet to use them in corporate worship. While none of the earliest elements will have survived the years unaltered from their original forms, the reader may detect most readily in this volume the contrast I have mentioned elsewhere in these prefaces between the playful brevity and expressive freedom that distinguish the elements first penned, and a more thorough, direct use of Scripture in more recent years. So, for instance, while the elements for Proper 15 and Second Sunday of Easter have recently passed beneath the same editor's pen, the description of forgiveness in the former as "the wild dance of prisoners escaping" will clearly reveal the newly minted pastor's exuberance, while a diminished use of paraphrase and a more direct iteration of the texts themselves (along with an increased, if occasional, indication in brackets of the texts in view) will feature in the more recent liturgies. This developmental detail may be of greater interest to the author than to the reader, but I offer it by way of explaining, once again, the sense in which the elements in this series will, for better or worse, speak in a variety of modes, moods, and tones, as I have attempted to remain within the bounds circumscribed by fresh expression and faithfulness, by spirit and truth.

It is perhaps more necessary to say a word about the title of this first and final volume, *Lightning from the East*. For the record, the reader would be very much mistaken to interpret this as an overture to Eastern religions, as though the Judeo-Christian tradition were not already "Eastern" enough. Rather, allusion is made to one of Jesus' apocalyptic sayings, one that in both Matthean and Lukan versions falls just outside the bounds of Year A, and with just the slightest adjustment on the part of the judicious preacher, might well speak on the First Sunday of Advent and at Thanksgiving:

> For as the lightning comes from the east and flashes as far as the west, so will be the coming of the Son of Man. (Matt 24:27; cf. Luke 17:24)

While I make no secret of my liberal (flexible) view of the boundaries of the lectionary and my (conservative) hope of including more apocalyptic texts, that expansive proposal is not the primary intent here. On the contrary, this eschatological image of the coming of the Son of Man with lightning from the east has been identified purely due to the ambiguity of the term itself and the way it is used here, which (taken together) typifies the vital ambiguity, the "already versus not yet" dialectic, that has long characterized both the church's Advent expectations and our understanding of eighth-day worship itself, that is, worship on "the Lord's Day" or "the day of the Lord." The ambiguous genitive has long been pregnant with eschatological expectation, and this expectation, it should be emphasized, is and shall ever be crucially characteristic of Sunday worship (on the Lord's Day) until the glorious consummation (the Day of the Lord). The same ambiguity, as I have mentioned before, attends the word *parousia*, which signals both the *presence* and the *coming* of the risen Lord Jesus. Thus, my aim in identifying this text, despite the bad form of transgressing ever so slightly the boundaries of Year A, is simply to express the eschatological hope that (ideally) permeates Christian worship in every tradition, Reformed or otherwise, namely, the hope of encountering the presence of the coming Christ on a day—the fast-approaching day—devoted to worship.

The word for lightning (Greek, *astrapé*), perhaps sufficiently "cognative" to redeem the term Easter from its pagan allusions, suggests a sudden flash of light rather than a gradual illumination, but the pattern and direction of this illumination from east to west suggests not so much an oddly horizontal bolt of electricity with a linearity that is hardly characteristic of such a phenomenon, but something more mundane, something that appears "as the world turns." Here again, we see such tensions widely expressed in the Church, as, for example, between different types or rates of conversion and sanctification: some are born again in a flash; others are plodding pilgrims whose awakening unfolds over years and even decades. Such tensions, as they relate to experiences of the Christian life, the presence of the Lord, and worship, should not be collapsed, but respected until "kingdom come."

Although I certainly do not intend to advance any thematic focus on lightning per se here, which would risk losing the sense of cyclical, existential illumination that forms an essential pole of the dialectic in question, it is nevertheless peculiar how comparatively few canonical references to lightning make their way into the RCL. Matthew's description (28:3) of the angel in the empty tomb is a rare exception (Easter, Year A), as is Jesus' vision of the fall of Satan (Luke 10:18; Proper 9, Year C). The plural form, "lightnings," occurs in an annual psalm selection for Christmas Day (ABC)—"His lightnings light up the world" (Ps 97:4)—which appears again on the Seventh Sunday in Easter, Year C. Also in Year C (and optionally in Proper 28, Year D), we encounter this laudatory phrase: "your lightnings lit up the world" (Ps 77:18; Proper 8, Year C). Otherwise, one must turn to Year D for the allusions to this majestic expression of the glory of God in the Psalms ("lightning" in 105:32; "lightnings" in 18:14; 135:7; 144:6). In Year B, an optional reference to the plural form arises in a speech from the whirlwind (Job 38:35; Proper 24), but the remaining references to lightning in Job (all in the singular) occur in the speech of Elihu (36:30, 32; 37:3, 11, 15; Transfiguration, Year D). Likewise, Year D alone includes the following (singular and plural) references to lightning in the prophets: Jer 10:13 (Christmas Day); Zech 9:14 (Proper 14); Nah 2:4 (Proper 27). Meanwhile, the following prophetic and apocalyptic references are nowhere included in either RCL or Year D: Jer 51:16; Ezek 1:13–14; 21:10, 28; Dan 10:6; Rev 4:5; 8:5; 11:19; 16:18.

I am not entirely sure what, if anything, one can conclude from this, except perhaps to note that, while the fearsome description of Mount

Sinai just prior to the Lord's utterance of the Ten Commandments did not quite make the cut (Exod 19:16; see Proper 6, where the Torah reading is limited to 19:2–8a), this important episode has been retained:

> When all the people witnessed the thunder and lightning, the sound of the trumpet, and the mountain smoking, they were afraid and trembled and stood at a distance, and said to Moses, "You speak to us, and we will listen; but do not let God speak to us, or we will die." (Exod 20:18–19; Proper 22, Year A; and 3rd Lent, Year B)

In other words, with the omission of so many references to theophanic lightning and with the selection of this particular passage that virtually institutes the preaching office while simultaneously pulling the plug on these alarming outbursts, the Church appears to be affirming this ancient preference that worship should not be disturbed—and the people should not be scared witless—by such displays of the divine glory. But I note this in passing, with no other aim than to invite fresh thoughts of the majesty, the power, and the glory of God, as well as the grace and mercy whereby the Lord restrains this power and glory for the protection and preservation of his people.

One final word on the titles in the *LERW* series: where no continuity of the imagery employed was originally deliberated or intended, it does appear in retrospect that a certain progression or "motion picture" befitting the dynamics of worship emerges when one considers the titles in sequence. If "lightning from the east" signals the approach of the risen Christ on the Lord's Day, the prospect of heaven standing open well describes the theater of glory in which the divine-human encounter of worship unfolds. Similarly eschatological and apocalyptic, "the joyful feast" alludes to the Word of God read and preached, as well as broken and shared in the foretaste of the wedding banquet of Christ and the Church. Finally, if the Word of God is to be made fully known, "greater attention" is needed, the phrase connoting a sort of beatific vision that arrests one's attention in worship with all senses firing. While the titles of these resources are no doubt somewhat trivial compared to the substance of their liturgical content, which I hope will find frequent use in public worship with genuinely doxological results, nevertheless, in the event that this hope is not realized and they fall into disuse for a time, then perhaps, if they are but shelved in sequence, their hopeful vision may yet be detected simply in titular form and remind the Church of these essentials of worship: the presence of the approaching Christ, the opening of heaven, the feeding on the Word, and the rapt contemplation of the revelation of God. Such a series of emphases is not meant to exclude or downplay the stress that must be laid on the Church's response to the Word by engaging in mission, an emphasis that gives direction to the invitations to the offering, the prayers of dedication, and the benedictions that feature in the first three volumes of this series. But, as I have tried to reiterate in my teaching of worship, it should remind the reader, especially the instinctively pragmatic reader, that in the grand scheme of things, mission is our temporary assignment; worship is our eternal vocation. Mission is for now; worship is forever.

—TMS
Dubuque, Iowa
July 31, 2013

Acknowledgments

ANY VOLUME OF LITURGICAL ELEMENTS FOR CHRISTIAN WORSHIP IN THE Reformed tradition must necessarily begin and end and be permeated throughout with thanksgiving and praise to the Triune God. *Soli Deo Gloria!* But while the Trinity has also determined, by virtue of the grace of God's revelation, incarnation, mission, and covenantal nature, to involve and enlist many saints in the ongoing ministry of the Word and the Spirit, and while there are innumerable agents of God's grace for whom I do give thanks at this juncture, I will confine myself to mentioning those whose roles loom largest in my admittedly porous memory.

First of all, and most instrumentally, I give thanks for the two congregations I have been blessed to serve as pastor and interim pastor, respectively, for it is these congregations that first gave voice and lent their communal "Amen" to these various elements, or something close to them: Central Presbyterian Church, Tarentum, Pennsylvania (1995–2000) and First Presbyterian Church, Titusville, New Jersey (2004–2008). In the case of Year D, it was the latter congregation that served as its testing ground, and the fruits of it have been apparent.

The gracious pedagogical comments of the late Dr. Lucy Rose of Columbia Seminary continue to be instructive each time I teach worship. The prayers of the Reverend Roy Henderson at Lansdowne Parish Church, Glasgow, UK, a fine wordsmith, fed me for a year's worth of Sundays abroad, while the leaders of the Late Late Service, also in Glasgow, challenged me by example to think through the words used in worship with painstaking care (1992–93). Dr. Fred Anderson's labors at Madison Avenue Presbyterian Church and his enormous contribution to the worship of the Presbyterian Church (USA) are well documented, and I am grateful for the encouragement he has offered in our few, brief, but memorable exchanges.

The shape of Lavon Bayler's resources, *Taught By Love*, *Led By Love*, and *Gathered By Love* (United Church Press), which I ran across in 1996 and have used on occasion, inspired the notion that I might be able to build a similar resource over time, but in a more Reformed voice and vein.

Dr. Richard Young, now at Orchard Park Presbyterian Church in the Buffalo, New York area, offered encouragement early on, and was a rare and delightful conversation partner as we were both serving in western Pennsylvania.

My professors at Princeton Seminary, specifically, Dr. James F. Kay (now Dean), Dr. Sally Brown, and visiting lecturer Dr. Hughes Oliphant Old (now Dean of Erskine Seminary's Institute for Reformed Worship) prompted more critical (and self-critical) thinking about liturgical concerns, and I am grateful for their instruction in seminars, in their pedagogy, and in their scholarship.

I am also grateful to the First Presbyterian Church, Topeka, Kansas, which has served as my "safe home" sanctuary for going on fifty years. I am especially grateful to the long line of ministers, musicians, and other saints who have served that congregation over the years, and maintained a highly esthetic doxology; the Reverend C. Michael Kuner, who once served the church as both Associate Pastor and later as Interim Head of Staff, is my brother-in-law and has served as a mentor for many years; Mike's wife and my sister, Jennifer Kuner, has often filled the sanctuary with her exquisite solo (and choral) contributions, carrying on the contralto reverberations our mother first put in motion there beginning in the 1940s. My brother Rob and his wife Julie have always been encouraging where my writing is concerned, while my sisters Jen and Claire have rendered such care to our aging mother as has eased my own mind considerably, and freed me to labor at such projects as this one. Ashley Smith, of Cleveland, Ohio, a Presbyterian elder who works with the Cleveland Youth Orchestra, Karen Smith of Oakmont, Pennsylvania, a frequent soprano soloist, and her mother (and Ashley's grandmother), Betty Hicks, a lifelong organist, have joined in or initiated numerous discussions of worship through the years, and one is ever mindful of key considerations in light thereof. Of course, I am most grateful that the Lord saw fit to bring me into the world through, and place me in the care of, two of the most loving and gracious parents a child could ever hope for: my mother Dorothy Herrick Slemmons and my late father Robert Sheldon

Slemmons. I continually give thanks, and I do so again now, that my parents raised us in the church: Sunday school, worship, youth choir, bell choir, youth groups, etc., every week whenever each was in session.

Finally, I give thanks for Victoria, for whom worship is, not just theory but in reality, the most joyous daily activity. She has graciously borne with me through the years in my labors on Year D and repeatedly confirmed its merits. I bless the LORD for her ministry of prayer, in song, and at the harp, for the sweetness of her voice and her spirit, and for the lovely sounds of her inspired psalm settings, to say nothing of all the other dimensions of the life of Christian marriage and friendship that we share in Christ. Come, LORD Jesus!

PART I

The Christmas Cycle
Advent—Christmas—Epiphany

First Sunday of Advent

Isaiah 2:1–5

Psalm 122

Romans 13:11–14

Matthew 24:36–44

IN PREPARATION FOR WORSHIP

Come and walk in the light of the Lord.
Let us go up to the house of our God,
that he may teach us his ways
and that we may walk in his paths.

CALL TO WORSHIP

Now is the moment to awake from sleep.
For salvation is nearer to us now than when we first came to believe.
> **Come, let us go up to the mountain of our God.**
> **For the night is far gone and the day is near.**

I was glad when they said to me,
"Let us go to the house of the Lord!"
> **We shall lay aside the works of darkness**
> **and put on the armor of light.**

Ask the Lord to show us the true way
and await God's word of instruction.
> **We shall put on the Lord Jesus Christ,**
> **and make no provision for sinful desires.**

Part I: The Christmas Cycle

Opening Prayer

Eternal God, we do not know when you will return for us, but we seek to be always vigilant. We do not understand all the ways in which you are already present, but we would be awakened and watch for you. Come quickly, Lord Jesus! Come soon! But until you come at the final consummation, steal among us this Lord's Day, as you have promised and as you have done for centuries, for the territory you survey is yours!

Call to Confession

To put on the Lord Jesus Christ as the armor of light entails a summons to an entirely new identity, according to which our conduct is completely honorable, with no allowance made for the gratification of the flesh. Let us exchange our former ways for the righteousness of God, by putting away the deeds of darkness, confessing our sins, and seeking and receiving the light of Christ.

OR

The Lord has a vision for all the peoples of the earth: that they should beat their swords into plowshares, and their spears into pruning hooks, to take what might be used for weapons and refashion them into tools of cultivation, production, prosperity, and peace. Let us confess, on behalf of the nations, the sinful economic imbalance that privileges wealth and warfare over the feeding of the poor and the care of those in need.

Prayer of Confession

God of righteousness and mercy, we confess we are so deeply engrossed in the cares of this world that we grow forgetful of eternal things. We are often tired, frustrated, and discouraged, seeking fulfillment in ways that are not your ways. We repent of all that displeases you and we forsake our former ways. Help us relinquish fruitless habits and receive a fresh outpouring of your Holy Spirit. Clothe us in Christ, we pray, for your glory!

OR

God of peace, we confess we are often so fearful of the growing needs around us that we seek to secure our own well-being at the expense of others. We give tacit approval to wars in foreign lands, knowing that the conflict will remain far off, little thinking of the suffering it brings or of the violence within our own cities, neighborhoods, and homes. Forgive us, O God, for our numb denial and our evasion of responsibility. Inspire us with your vision of the coming kingdom of peace, and give us courage to live as though it is already among us, for indeed, if you are among us, your kingdom cannot be far behind!

Declaration of Forgiveness

The wise and vigilant are always ready for the coming day of the Lord. Salvation is near, nearer now than it has ever been. Judgment is coming, but those who make good use of the time will be spared the judgment if they keep faith in the One who has been judged and deemed worthy, Christ Jesus, our gracious Savior, himself a glorious garment of light who imparts a renewed mind, a grateful heart, and a new identity that conforms to his image. Turn and receive the innumerable blessings of Christ this day, and know that in Christ you are forgiven.

Presentation of Tithes and Offerings

Seek the good of the house of the Lord. Pray for the peace of the people of God. Let us render our gifts to the Spirit of God, and see what the Lord will do!

Prayer of Dedication

Though we cannot compare our charity to yours, it makes us glad, O God, to imitate your giving. Your blessings abound, they fill and surround us. As you have freely bound yourself to the redemption of your chosen people and of this troubled world, so in freedom, gratitude, and love, we commit these gifts to you. May this offering be pleasing to you as our testimony of trust, our act of adoration.

The Blessing

Be arrayed in light and guard against temptation.
Be clothed in Christ and watch for his coming.
Be filled with the Spirit, and the One who created you
will make you faithful, fruitful, and exceedingly glad.

Second Sunday of Advent

Isaiah 11:1–10
Psalm 72:1–7, 18–19
Romans 15:4–13
Matthew 3:1–12

In Preparation for Worship

Eternal God, you know
when our deeds are faithful and when they are not,
when our thoughts are truthful and when they are not,
when our words are loving and when they are not.
We would be more like Jesus in all areas of life.
We come to learn your ways.

Call to Worship

Let the earth be filled with the knowledge of the Lord.
Let us praise God together, with one voice.
> **As the waters cover the depths of the sea,**
> **so let our hearts be filled with love.**
> **For we have seen God's mercy in our Lord Jesus Christ!**

Let all people repent, fear the Lord, and prosper.
May all nations turn to God, that the earth may be filled with peace.
> **We await the coming of our righteous King.**
> **For the Son of God shall lead us in the ways of truth.**

Blessed be the Lord, the God of Israel,
Who alone does wondrous things!

Blessed be the glorious name of God forever.
May the glory of the Lord fill the whole earth.

Opening Prayer

Spirit of the Living God, we look for your promises to be fulfilled, for your peace to reign over us, for justice to be done, that we might live as you would have us live. We want our children to know you, to grow in your Spirit, to delight in your ways. Come, Lord Jesus! We long for your kingdom. We thirst for your grace.

Call to Confession

Do not presume anything when it comes to salvation. But let everyone bear fruit that is worthy of repentance. Let everyone's deeds give evidence of a pure heart. And where our actions or affections are false, let us, in honesty and humility, confess this to God.

Prayer of Confession

Sovereign God, we are told that your kingdom has come near. We confess this confuses us, for we all too rarely perceive it. We are dismayed at the sin we see in the world and we tremble to name the sin that dwells in our hearts. We are told to repent, yet sometimes we lack even the desire to change. Forgive us, O God. Have mercy on us and transform us, that we may with joy look forward to your coming. Draw us into your silent, loving, merciful grace, in the name of Jesus.

Declaration of Forgiveness

Christ Jesus embodies divine wisdom, knowledge, and truth for God's covenant people, in order to confirm and fulfill the promises made to our ancestors in former times and in order that all nations might glorify God for his mercy. Therefore, be steadfast in faith and take courage from our merciful Savior, who forgives all our sins, and whose desire it is that we should glorify God as one. Praise the Lord, all you nations! Let all the peoples praise the holy name of our Lord!

Second Sunday of Advent 9

Presentation of Tithes and Offerings

We are servants of the One who judges with righteousness on behalf of the poor and with equity on behalf of the meek of the earth. So let the Lord's ways become our ways. Let us gird ourselves with justice and use the authority that we have in Christ to give deliverance to the needy, to shower blessings on those around us, and to share our gifts as is pleasing to God.

Prayer of Dedication

Holy and Blessed One, we offer you this modest portion of our countless blessings. May they be used as you so desire. May their administration be in accordance with your spirit of love and your light of justice, that the nations might see it and give you praise. We ask this in Jesus' name.

The Blessing

Trust in the Lord Jesus Christ to rise and reign over you,
the God of hope to fill you with joy and peace,
and the power of the Holy Spirit
to grant you life and hope in abundance,
from this day forth and forevermore.

Third Sunday of Advent

Isaiah 35:1–10

Psalm 146:5–10 OR Luke 1:47–55

James 5:7–10

Matthew 11:2–11

In Preparation for Worship

You are the author of such great reversals,
who makes the desert bloom
and the scorching sand become a pool of refreshing water.
Show us the righteous way you have made for reformed sinners.
Prepare us, that we may walk that holy way!

Call to Worship

Be strong, O people, and do not fear.
Here is your God, come to save!
> Let the eyes of the blind be opened, O God.
> Let the ears of the deaf be unstopped.

Strengthen our weak hands, O Lord.
Make firm our feeble and weary frames!
> Let the lame leap for joy, O God.
> Let the mute break forth in song.

Come, O ransomed of the Lord, and joyfully return to Zion.
May your heads be crowned with everlasting glory!
> Let sorrow and sighing cease.
> Rejoice and be glad at the presence of our God!

Third Sunday of Advent 11

OPENING PRAYER

Holy God, you are the Maker of earth, sea, and sky. You have done great things for us, for you give food to the hungry, justice to the oppressed, and love to the unloved. Indeed, you keep faith forever! Happy are those who hope in you, who trust in you to provide.

CALL TO CONFESSION

Be patient, beloved, until the coming of the Lord. As a farmer awaits the growth of a precious crop, waiting for both the early and the latter rains, so we too must be patient. Let us not grumble against one another, for the Judge is standing at the very doors. Therefore, let us prepare the way for the Lord's coming by means of repentance and the humble confession of our sins.

PRAYER OF CONFESSION

Almighty God, look with favor upon the lowliness of your servants. For we confess that, in our pride, we have exalted ourselves and manipulated others; in greed and fear, we have tried to stave the emptiness of our hearts and denied our inability to control our circumstances. Forgive us, Lord, for indeed, we are hungry and long to be filled with good things; we are weak, and we look to you for strength. Merciful God, look with favor on the lowliness of your servants!

DECLARATION OF FORGIVENESS

The LORD lifts up those who are bowed down. The LORD sets the prisoners free. Those who fear the LORD from generation to generation will be shown mercy, but the way of the wicked will be brought to ruin. Rejoice, O people, in God your Savior, for the grace of the Lord is with you!

PRESENTATION OF TITHES AND OFFERINGS

The LORD brings good news to the poor! But how shall God do so unless Christ's proclaiming church becomes the herald of the good tidings and devotes its tithes and offerings, its collective heart and soul to showing forth Christ's kingdom and its joyful order of life? Let us demonstrate to the world, by the grace of God, the new creation into which we are being formed: a newborn body of Christ, a fellowship of love within this broken and hurting world.

Prayer of Dedication

Let our gifts serve your glory, O Lord, that the world might remember you are a giver of many blessings. Let our offerings be of service to you, O Christ, that the suffering might be touched by your tender mercies. Let our lives be open to your spirit of love, that we may show the light of your grace to all. By your blessing may these gifts, O Holy God, strengthen in love those who give them and those who receive them.

The Blessing

May the Lord watch over and uphold you.
May Jesus reign over you and set you free for giving.
May the Spirit fulfill your hope for love, your longing for life,
and give you great joy in Christ your Savior.

Fourth Sunday of Advent

Isaiah 7:10–16
Psalm 80:1–7, 17–19
Romans 1:1–7
Matthew 1:18–25

In Preparation for Worship

Gracious God, we rejoice that you are with us.
Savior of the world, we take heart that you are born for us.
Holy Spirit, conceive in us the One in whom
we must be born anew,
that by the gift of your grace
and through the life of discipleship,
we might be enlisted to bring about the obedience of faith
among the nations, for the sake of your most holy name.

Call to Worship

Turn to the Lord, the Most High God,
enthroned on the wings of heaven's angels.
> **Hear us, holy Shepherd.**
> **Come and lead your flock.**
Call upon the Lord, the God of hosts,
whose strength has saved us from sin and shame.
> **Restore us, redeeming God.**
> **Let your face shine that we may be saved!**

Call upon the name of the Lord,
who gives us life and eternal salvation!
> **Regard us, everlasting God.**
> **Show us your glory and we will not turn away!**

Opening Prayer

Loving God, you have spoken to us through your angels and prophets, heralding the gospel news that salvation from sin has come to us through your Son Jesus Christ. We thank you and praise you that we have nothing to fear, since in Christ Jesus you have come to us and you are with us, even in our present condition, that we might receive grace, learn obedience, and grow in your spirit of holiness.

Call to Confession

Do not think that God is slow to bless. But ask the Lord for the deepest and highest: the removal of sin and the gift of a holy life. For God is sure to give it, and in truth, in Christ, he has already done so.

Prayer of Confession

Holy God, who has set us apart from the world to bear the light of Christ within it, we confess that we have failed to live obedient lives. We frequently turn from you, fail to call out to you, and fear to ask for or receive the wondrous signs of your presence and the righteous blessings that you so freely give. Forgive us, O Lord, and let not the darkness overwhelm us. But shine upon, within, and among us! Let your saving light be seen in the midst of your people, for the sake of the nations, and for the glory of your name.

Declaration of Forgiveness

The gift of God is far greater than we can imagine. The Christ child born for us is "God with us." He himself puts an end to sin and inaugurates an entirely new creation. For in Christ we learn to refuse the evil and choose the good. Trust in the Lord, therefore, through whose grace we are forgiven, in whom we are chosen, and by whom we are sent to teach faith to the nations. Praise be to God!

Presentation of Tithes and Offerings

We belong to Christ Jesus, the Son of God and Savior of God's people. Therefore, since we belong to Christ, who shares everything with us, what loss could we possibly suffer by sharing all we have with Christ? Let us offer our gifts to God.

Prayer of Dedication

Let your hand be upon these gifts, O God, upon those who give, and upon those who are unable to give, even as your hand is upon the one at your right hand. Whether we are endowed with many gifts or few, we are incalculably rich, for we belong to you and to your chosen One, Jesus Christ, whose name we would bless this day and forever.

The Blessing

Receive new life in the light of Christ.
Refuse evil and choose the good.
Ask the Lord and you will surely receive refreshing from the Holy Spirit,
by whom our Savior became incarnate in the flesh,
and by whom he has also been raised from the dead.

Christmas, First Proper (ABC)
Christmas Eve

Isaiah 9:2–7

Psalm 96

Titus 2:11–14

Luke 2:1–14 (15–20)

In Preparation for Worship

Wonderful Counselor, Everlasting Father,
you are zealous for your people who are burdened and oppressed.
Free us from tyranny and enslavement to sin.
Fill us with joy at the birth of your Son,
at the gift of our Savior, the chosen One.

Call to Worship

All the gods of the people are idols.
But the Lord made the heavens.
> **Hear, O nations, of the glory of God!**

Worship the Lord in holy splendor.
Let all the earth tremble at the presence of the Lord.
> **Hear, O nations: the Lord our God reigns!**

Great is the Lord and greatly to be praised.
The Lord is to be revered above all gods.
> **Hear, O nations: God is coming!**
> **The Lord is coming to judge the earth!**

Opening Prayer

Shine your great light, O Prince of Peace. Scatter the deep darkness of this world. Exercise your authority, O Mighty God. May your reign ever increase. Subdue the ruler of the nations, O Lord of hosts. We long for your righteousness, your endless peace!

Call to Confession

The grace of God has appeared to all, bringing salvation! Indeed, this very grace instructs us, training us to renounce impiety and worldly passions, and to live self-controlled, upright, and godly lives, even as we await the blessed hope and the manifestation of the glory of our great God and Savior, Jesus Christ. As his disciples, tutored by his grace, let us renounce sin, impiety, unfaith, and all the evils from which Christ has come to deliver us.

Prayer of Confession

Everlasting Father, we confess that our hearts are not always true, our deeds not always pure, our desires not always in keeping with your holy and righteous will. For we have shown greater zeal for securing our own comfort than for alleviating the suffering around us. We see the world's overwhelming problems, and we soon despair of doing any good at all. Forgive us for our weak faith, our feeble hope, our lack of self-control. We ask your grace and mercy; for indeed your righteous wisdom in sending Jesus Christ is not punitive or vindictive, but is the tender remedy of which we, and this world, stand in such great need.

Declaration of Forgiveness

Hear the good news! Jesus Christ, our great God and Savior, has given himself in order to redeem us from all iniquity and to purify for himself a people of his own who are zealous for good deeds. Therefore, give praise to God for the purifying work that Christ Jesus has done on our behalf, and show forth his redeeming grace with works of love done in his name. Praise the Lord!

Presentation of Tithes and Offerings

Let the heavens be glad, and let the earth rejoice; for the Lord has blessed us and increased our joy. Let us rejoice before the Lord, as with joy at the harvest, singing, "Glory to God in the highest heaven, and on earth peace and good will!" With glad and generous hearts let us offer our gifts to God.

Prayer of Dedication

Holy Spirit of God, who conceived our precious Savior, who descended at his baptism, who raised him from the dead: you have endowed your people with many gifts. Rather than asking for new ones, as the world urges us to do in this season, help us put to fruitful use those you have already given us. Inspire us to use them in new ways for the glory of our Sovereign, Christ Jesus, your Son.

The Blessing

Treasure this good news of great joy in your heart
and share it with all people:
Jesus Christ is the Lord,
born as a sign to you of God's marvelous love and mighty glory;
he is the Prince of Peace,
who will establish and uphold endless peace
with justice and righteousness
from this time onward and forevermore.
Go, and be ambassadors of this peace,
in the name of Jesus Christ.

Christmas, Second Proper (ABC)
Christmas Morning

Isaiah 62:6–12
Psalm 97
Titus 3:4–7
Luke 2:(1–7) 8–20

IN PREPARATION FOR WORSHIP

O God, in the birth of the One who gives rebirth,
in the spirit of the One who pours out the Spirit,
we see your mercy, we know your lovingkindness,
we find such hope of knowing lasting love in this world,
such hope of eternal life.
In this reverent hope we seek you,
in the face of Jesus, God our Savior.

CALL TO WORSHIP [Psalm 97]

The LORD is king! Let the earth rejoice;
let the many coastlands be glad!
> Clouds and thick darkness are all around him;
> righteousness and justice are the foundation of his throne.

Fire goes before him, and consumes his adversaries on every side.
> His lightnings light up the world; the earth sees and trembles.

The mountains melt like wax before the LORD,

before the Lord of all the earth.
> The heavens proclaim his righteousness;
> and all the peoples behold his glory.

All worshipers of images are put to shame,
those who make their boast in worthless idols;
all gods bow down before him.
> Zion hears and is glad, and the towns of Judah rejoice,
> because of your judgments, O God.

For you, O Lord, are most high over all the earth;
you are exalted far above all gods.
> The Lord loves those who hate evil;
> he guards the lives of his faithful;
> he rescues them from the hand of the wicked.

Light dawns for the righteous,
and joy for the upright in heart.
> Rejoice in the Lord, O you righteous,
> and give thanks to his holy name!

or [see Isaiah 62:6–12]

The Lord has proclaimed to the end of the earth:
"See, your salvation comes."
> His reward is with him,
> his recompense before him.

"Go through the gates; prepare the way for my people."
> Build up the highway; clear it of stones.

"My daughter Zion shall be called,
'Sought Out, A City Not Forsaken.'"
> Come, let us worship the Lord.

Opening Prayer

Holy One, your prophets tell us to give you no rest until you establish Jerusalem and make it renowned throughout the earth; indeed, you have proclaimed to the end of the earth: "See, your salvation comes; you shall be called, 'The Holy People, The Redeemed of the Lord.'" Build up, therefore, this people whom you have gathered. Lead us through your gates and draw us to yourself! Raise your royal banner over your people, that we may find ourselves in the presence of the new standard for humankind, Jesus the Christ, your Son, whom you have sent in order to save sinners and to establish your righteous and peaceful reign on earth. In his name we pray.

Call to Confession

The good news of great joy is news of a Savior; this is indeed good news, for we stand in need of saving, of deliverance! Although we may not fully understand this gift in the moment it is given or received, and we may not even fully understand how much we need it, we can nevertheless make a good beginning by acknowledging our need and that our need is attributable to the problem of sin. In this way, we will surely come to, among many other good things, a greater appreciation of the good news of great joy that is meant for all people. Let us confess our sin to God.

Prayer of Confession

We confess, O Lord, that like children we are often afraid of the dark—whether it be the dark of winter or of cruel deeds done, the dark of mood or dejected spirit, the dark of the eye gone dim and downcast, so that the inner life is closed off and begins to die. Yet your heavenly messengers have proclaimed: Do not be afraid! They have announced the arrival of the Light of the World! You have looked upon the world of sinners with unmerited favor, and your heavenly choir sings of your glory in the highest heaven and of peace on earth, good will among your favored people: friends, family, strangers, former enemies. Forgive us, O Lord, for indulging fear and accommodating the culture of death, for trembling at whatever darkness we perceive or imagine. Fill us with your radiant light! Let your face shine upon us, as we see in the face of your Son Jesus Christ the face of all things made new! In his holy name we pray.

Declaration of Forgiveness

Hear again the good news: Our gracious God knows the effect of sin on the human creature. This is why he forgives and redeems: so that we might learn the obedience we have not shown in former times, and so that we might be made ready for every good work. For we ourselves were once foolish, led astray, slaves to various passions and pleasures. But when the goodness and lovingkindness of God our Savior appeared, he saved us, not because of any works of righteousness that we had done, but according to his mercy, through the water of rebirth and renewal by the Holy Spirit. This Spirit he poured out on us richly through Jesus Christ, our Savior, so that, having been justified by his grace, we might become heirs according to the hope of eternal life.

Presentation of Tithes and Offerings

As the Lord made known to the shepherds the good news of the Savior's birth, and as the shepherds made known to Joseph and Mary what had been told them by angels about the child Jesus, let us in turn offer our gifts, that the joyful news may be made known in our day and that this generation may come to share our hope and give glory to God in the highest.

Prayer of Dedication

Sovereign Lord, let the heavens proclaim your righteousness and all the peoples behold your glory! May those who testify to your saving goodness never be silent, but may our life together and this outpouring of our hearts tell the world of your lovingkindness, that the hearts of those who have not yet received your Son might melt like wax before you, and that they might know rebirth and renewal through the gift of the Spirit and in the name of Jesus Christ, our Savior.

The Blessing

May the light of Christ that has dawned upon the righteous
ever fill your hearts with joy
and crown you with the hope of eternal life!

Christmas, Third Proper (ABC)
Christmas Day

Isaiah 52:7–10

Psalm 98

Hebrews 1:1–4 (5–12)

John 1:1–14

IN PREPARATION FOR WORSHIP

You, O God, speak through the wind;
fire and flame serve as your messengers.
Yet, how far above the angels is your firstborn
that all the angels worship him!
Fill our hearts and minds with the One
of whom all creation sings,
that we might join in giving praise
to Jesus Christ, our God in human flesh!

CALL TO WORSHIP [Psalm 98]

O sing to the LORD a new song,
for he has done marvelous things.
> **His right hand and his holy arm
> have gotten him victory.**

The LORD has made known his victory;
he has revealed his vindication in the sight of the nations.

> **He has remembered his steadfast love**
> **and faithfulness to the house of Israel.**
> **All the ends of the earth have seen the victory of our God.**
> Make a joyful noise to the LORD, all the earth;
> **break forth into joyous song and sing praises.**
> Sing praises to the LORD with the lyre,
> with the lyre and the sound of melody.
> **With trumpets and the sound of the horn**
> **make a joyful noise before the King, the LORD.**
> Let the sea roar, and all that fills it;
> the world and those who live in it.
> **Let the floods clap their hands;**
> let the hills sing together for joy at the presence of the LORD,
> for he is coming to judge the earth.
> **He will judge the world with righteousness,**
> **and the peoples with equity.**

OR [Isaiah 52:9–10]

> Break forth together into singing,
> you ruins of Jerusalem;
> **for the LORD has comforted his people,**
> **he has redeemed Jerusalem.**
> The LORD has bared his holy arm
> before the eyes of all the nations;
> **and all the ends of the earth shall see**
> **the salvation of our God.**

Opening Prayer

O God, you who have spoken to generations of the faithful in many and various ways, through angels, prophets, and apostles, we thank you for Jesus Christ, your Word in the flesh, through whom you have spoken worlds into being and whom you have appointed heir of all things. Your Son reflects your glory, embodies your perfect character, and sustains all things by his powerful word. As we rejoice in his birth for our salvation, grant that each one here may receive him, trust in his name, and find in him the full measure of truth and grace to become your beloved child in accordance with your sovereign will; in Jesus' name we pray.

Call to Confession

The supreme gladness and joy of Jesus Christ, the anointed one, derives from his love of righteousness, as well as his hatred of wickedness. It is this separation, not from sinners whom he came to save, but from the spiritual source of darkness, sin, and evil, that distinguishes the light of Christ from every other light; and he desires to share his holy light with all God's children. Let us, in the confession of sin, renounce wickedness and express our desire for the righteousness that Christ alone can give.

Prayer of Confession

Lord Jesus, full of grace and truth, in you is our true life, for your life is the light that the darkness cannot overcome. We confess that, though you have come to your own, bearing the Father's glory, we have hidden from your glory and have often failed to receive you; when in our sinful foolishness we cut ourselves off from the fullness of your gracious will, we wasted away in the darkness of isolation. Forgive us, O Lord, and restore us to your saving presence; refresh our spirits with the good news of your peace and the happy realization that our God does indeed reign over us, for your glory and for our inexpressible joy!

Declaration of Forgiveness

Christ's throne is forever and ever, and his righteous scepter is that of the kingdom of God. For when Jesus made purification for sins, he sat down at the right hand of the Majesty on high, whence the good news was sent forth, announcing salvation. As the beautiful messengers have proclaimed, and as the watchful sentinels have sung: our God reigns and we have seen his glory! Hear and believe this good news: We have peace with God and with one another through our Lord Jesus Christ. Praise the Lord!

Presentation of Tithes and Offerings

In the beginning, the Word of God founded the earth and the heavens, and yet these things are temporary; they will perish, but God will remain; they will all wear out like clothing, but Jesus Christ is the same yesterday, today, and forever. Let us therefore direct our gifts to the one who endures, that by the will and power of the Holy Spirit, something enduring might be done with them, for the glory of our triune God.

Prayer of Dedication

Triune God, all things have come into being through you, and without you not one thing has come into being. Receive and bless these humble gifts, that, as we return them to you, their use may conform to your design and testify to the true light, the gracious life, and the redeeming love of Jesus Christ, in whose name we pray.

The Blessing

May the true light, which enlightens everyone,
abide with you and
continue to make its way in the world through you,
as you bear witness to the love of God
in Christ Jesus our Lord.

First Sunday after Christmas

Isaiah 63:7–9
Psalm 148
Hebrews 2:10–18
Matthew 2:13–23

IN PREPARATION FOR WORSHIP

Holy and Eternal Light,
illumine our dreams; flood our vision;
guide us through darkness, danger, and decision;
fill us with the knowledge of your kingdom,
and spread your wings of love
to the ends of the earth.

CALL TO WORSHIP [see Psalm 148]

Praise the LORD from the highest heavens!
Heavenly hosts and angels, praise him!
> **Let them praise the name of the LORD,**
> **for he commanded and they were created.**

Praise the LORD from the earth,
and from the ocean's very depths!
> **All peoples and rulers, old and young together,**
> **praise the name of the LORD.**

Let us recount the gracious deeds of the LORD,
because of all he has done for us.

For his gracious acts and the great favor he has shown us, praise the Lord!

Opening Prayer

O God our Creator, for whom and through whom all things exist, we join our voices with the whole created order in praise of your name alone. For your glory is above earth and heaven, and you have raised up a horn for your faithful people. Indeed, it is no messenger or angel, but your presence—Immanuel, Jesus Christ, "God with us"—who has saved your people. Therefore, we welcome your presence and look forward to the consummation, when you will be fully and finally with us, and we with you in glory.

Call to Confession

Scripture affirms that Jesus, though without sin, had to become like us in every other respect, that he might be a merciful and faithful high priest, able to make a sacrifice of atonement for our sins. Because he himself was tested by what he suffered, he is able to help those who are being tested. Therefore, let us confess our sins to God, affirming our faith in Jesus Christ and his power to do what he was sent to do.

Prayer of Confession

O Lord our Deliverer, as you rescued Israel from slavery and called the child Jesus out of Egypt, so too you have called your children out of their distress. We confess that we, your people, have shown you disloyalty and dealt falsely with you amidst the competing pressures of this world. Yet, we remember your gracious deeds; for in every generation, you have loved and pitied, redeemed and carried your children when they could not help themselves. Have mercy on us, O God, in keeping with all your praiseworthy acts in ages past. Show us favor and forgive us, according to the abundance of your steadfast love, for we place our trust in you and in your Son Jesus Christ, in whose name we pray.

Declaration of Forgiveness

Friends, hear the good news: Jesus Christ, the pioneer of our salvation, was perfected through what he suffered, in order to bring many children to glory; further, the one who sanctifies us and we who are sanctified all have one Father. For this reason Jesus is not ashamed to call us his brothers and sisters. Since, therefore, he shares our flesh and blood, he himself has, through death, destroyed the one who has the power of death, and freed those who all their lives have been held in slavery by the fear of death. Know, therefore, that our greatest fears, our greatest enemies, have been defeated by Jesus Christ, in whom we are forgiven, joyful, courageous, and free!

Presentation of Tithes and Offerings

The gifts of the wise were delivered, despite Herod's massacre of many children in his plot to destroy the child born King of the Jews. Surely, although the family of faith is still surrounded by the vestiges of evil forces and tyranny in the world, the ministry of grace and giving goes on; the worship of the Christ shall never end. Let us pay homage to Jesus with our gifts.

Prayer of Dedication

Lord God of Israel, let your name be proclaimed in the midst of the great congregation, and let the name of Jesus be praised throughout the earth and in the highest heavens. Let your children exult in your praiseworthy acts of mercy and redemption; and may these benefactions testify to the great favor you have shown us, and to the grace you have shown the world in sending Jesus Christ to set us free. Bless these gifts, that they, with the whole creation, may proclaim the good news!

The Blessing

Through death, Jesus has destroyed the one
who has the power of death, that is, the devil,
and has set free those who all their lives
have been enslaved by the fear of death.

Go, therefore, free from the fear of death,
free from the power of death,
and free to live and pray, to worship and witness
to the praise of God's glory in Jesus Christ.

Second Sunday after Christmas (ABC)

Jeremiah 31:7–14

Psalm 147:12–20

Ephesians 1:3–14

John 1:(1–9) 10–18

In Preparation for Worship

Gather us to yourself, O Christ our foundation,
that we may set all our hopes on you and live to praise your glory.
For in you we know all the riches of grace;
in you we shall trust for the fullness of time.

Call to Worship

The Lord calls to the ends of the earth:
Return to me, O my people! And I shall lead you home!
> **Spread the word to every corner of the earth.**
> **Sing out with gladness, that all may hear.**

Join the great company of those whom God calls!
See! They are radiant with the goodness of the Lord!
> **Save, O Lord, this remnant of your people!**
> **Hear our cries as loud shouts of praise!**

The word of the Lord is swift and sure:
All who come will be satisfied with my bounty!
> **God has redeemed us from the power of sin.**
> **Praise God, who has turned our mourning into joy!**

Opening Prayer

Blessed God, according to your exceeding kindness, we have been sealed with your Holy Spirit, marked as your own. Renew our apprehension of your wondrous promises; deepen our appreciation of your pledge of redemption; lighten our hearts once again with the good news of your grace so freely given, by which we are destined for adoption as your children and joined eternally with Christ Jesus our Lord.

Call to Confession

Our cries to God for help are heard by God as praise. Our weeping and lamentation to the Lord meet with God's comfort and consolation. What better way to declare God's worth to a sinful world than to show, in confession, that we trust in God for mercy, even as we hold God's justice in reverence and awe? Let us bow to our Holy and Sovereign God and confess our sin.

Prayer of Confession

Eternal Word, we confess we largely fail to comprehend you. Light of the world, we admit we have willfully hidden from you. God in the flesh, we concede we have neglected to receive you, as we should, in those whose needs are great. Forgive our innumerable sins, O Lord, and be gracious to us. Impart your wisdom to our dull, foolish minds; pierce the darkness in our hearts with your penetrating light and quicken us with love for the Beloved One, Jesus Christ, for neighbors, for strangers, and for everything that breathes in your good creation!

Declaration of Forgiveness

In Christ we have redemption, the forgiveness of our trespasses, through the blood of Jesus, shed on the cross. Though all the powers of sin and evil are too strong for us, Christ our Strength has rescued us with godly power and righteous obedience. Let the young rejoice and sing! Let the aged celebrate and be glad! In Christ Jesus, our saving Lord, we are forgiven, renewed, and restored!

Presentation of Tithes and Offerings

We have received so much from God's fullness, and from Christ Jesus, the Word made flesh: grace upon grace, grace beyond measure! In gratitude for the Lord's lavish generosity, let us be likewise generous, bestowing our gifts, even as we raise full hearts in love and thanksgiving to God!

Prayer of Dedication

Your light, your word, your life, O Lord, you have given to us in abundance. You have adopted us as your children; you have willed us, with Christ, your kingdom, your great estate. Therefore, we have nothing to lose by giving, but every joy to gain, for your promises are true forever. We are yours, Giver of all, as are these gifts. May we ever be responsive and obedient to your Spirit! May we always know the true worth in which you hold us, even as we live in the loving light of Christ.

The Blessing

May the Spirit of Truth fill you with wisdom.
May the Anointed of God shower you with light.
May the Creator of all inspire each decision,
and the angels watch over you, each day and night!

Epiphany (ABC)

Isaiah 60:1–6
Psalm 72:1–7, 10–14
Ephesians 3:1–12
Matthew 2:1–12

In Preparation for Worship

Creator of all,
who concealed the mystery for many ages
and finally revealed your eternal purpose in Christ Jesus our Lord,
prepare us to receive you and to perceive your wisdom
in wondrous array through your singular, holy Word.

Call to Worship

Come, O nations, to the light of Christ Jesus.
O rulers of the peoples, pay tribute to the Lord.
> Arise and shine, for your light has come.
> For the mystery of Christ has been revealed!

If darkness should cover the whole earth,
the Lord will arise upon you.
> Clouds and thick darkness surround the peoples.
> But the people of God shall see the glory of the Lord!

See, O Lord, how your people come to you.
See and be radiant, that your children may draw near.
> Proclaim the praise of Jesus our Lord!
> For the mystery of Christ is revealed!

Opening Prayer

We bless you, O God, for the glorious revelation of Christ Jesus, the Shepherd of your people, the Savior of our souls. Lift up your countenance upon us, let your bright dawn break over us, that we might worship and adore you as you alone deserve.

Call to Confession

Do not be proud or rely on your strength. Do not lose heart, but draw near to the Lord. For the Lord delivers the needy when they call. God pities the weak, rescues the humble, and helps the one who has no helper. Let us confess our sin in the presence of our God, to whom we have access through faith in Christ Jesus.

Prayer of Confession

We confess, O God, that we are often afraid. We have attached ourselves to the things of this world, and thus we live in fear of losing our comforts, our possessions, our influence, our positions. We are slow to trust that you desire to give us something far greater than we can ask for or imagine. We are slower still to make a new beginning, to receive you humbly, for you come to meet us with a humility far deeper, with a truth more humbling, than we can ever understand. Forgive us, O God, and accept our confession. For we have no other hope than our hope in you.

Declaration of Forgiveness

Be bold and confident and have faith in the Lord! He who was worshipped by rich kings and poor shepherds regards you as precious in his sight. Christ Jesus our Lord, our Good Shepherd King, shall make righteousness flourish and peace abound for you who seek the glory of the Lord. Know that in Jesus Christ you are forgiven, and be at peace.

Presentation of Tithes and Offerings

The wealth of the nations belongs to the Lord, the abundance of the earth and the sea! Therefore, it is fitting that we pay homage to our Messiah, with gifts of devotion and works of love.

Prayer of Dedication

O Shepherd of Israel, King of the Jews, you are our joy, our eternal treasure, for by your grace you have invited us, unworthy though we are, to be fellow heirs with you, members of the same body, sharers in the promises that God made from of old. Therefore, to you who offered yourself for us, we offer a portion of the boundless riches you have graciously shared with us. Receive these tributes to your righteous goodness, and use them, we pray, for your glory.

The Blessing

Bend your will to the will of God.
Resolve in your heart to glorify the Lord.
Ever seek to serve Jesus Christ in the power of the Holy Spirit.
For the riches of heaven and the blessings of the Lord are at your disposal as you minister in his name.

First Sunday after Epiphany
Ordinary Time 1 *(Baptism of the Lord)*

Isaiah 42:1–9

Psalm 29

Acts 10:34–43

Matthew 3:13–17

In Preparation for Worship

Lord of glory, give strength to your people.
Mighty God, bless us with peace.
The coastlands await your justice, your teaching.
Bathe us all in your righteousness.

Call to Worship

You have heard, O people, that God is not partial.
The Lord does not want any to perish.
> **Truly, anyone who fears the Lord**
> **and does what is right is acceptable to God!**

Therefore, come and hear again the good news of God's peace,
the message that Christ Jesus came preaching.
> **Truly, Christ is Lord of all,**
> **ordained to judge the living and the dead.**

Therefore, come and bear witness to Christ.
Testify to his goodness and believe in his name!

> Jesus is the One anointed
> to heal, to save, to rule, and to serve!

Opening Prayer

O Lord our God, who stretched out the heavens, who fills the earth, who gives life and breath to all who live in them: place your Holy Spirit upon us and within us, that we might faithfully and fearlessly serve you in the name of your beloved Son, the righteous One, Christ the Lord.

Call to Confession

All the prophets testify concerning the Christ that everyone who believes in him receives forgiveness through his name. As the heavenly Father baptized and anointed Jesus with the Holy Spirit and gave him power to heal all those oppressed by sin and evil, let us therefore, in faith and trust, humbly confess our sins.

Prayer of Confession

Merciful Savior, we confess we are weak, fragile, faint, and vulnerable to many temptations. We regret our past sins and often entertain dread of what the future holds. Where we have done harm, give healing and restoration. Where we have been cruel, give us hearts for compassion. Where we have been selfish, renew our love and give us an eagerness to share, so that your fulfillment of all righteousness might be seen in our midst, and we might look forward with joy to the promise of each day.

Declaration of Forgiveness

You know the message, sent by God, telling of reconciliation and peace through Christ Jesus, who is Lord of all! Jesus came doing the will of God, but he was put to death on the cross. Nevertheless, God raised Jesus on the third day and allowed him to appear to his disciples, that his saving work might be proclaimed and believed in every nation. Thus, this good news is now proclaimed to you—indeed, it is intended for you: in the name of Jesus Christ, you are forgiven!

Presentation of Tithes and Offerings

In his earthly ministry Jesus was quiet but determined, full of tenderness for the wounded and respect for the smoldering hope of the humble. Let us learn to imitate the earthly ministry of our Lord Jesus Christ through the godly administration of our gifts, for in Christ God has given us as a light to the nations, and the coastlands await the saving news of the gospel!

Prayer of Dedication

With each small offering, O Spirit of Christ, hear our sighs of surrender, of peace, of recognition that the former things have come to pass and it is time for you to do a new thing. Receive these outpourings, O Lord our God, and bless their use, that through them the blind and those bound in darkness might see your marvelous light and know freedom in the truth of Christ Jesus and in the Spirit of the Lord.

The Blessing

The Lord has called you to righteousness,
taken you by the hand,
and promised to keep you.
So be led by the Spirit,
in the wisdom of Christ,
for the glory of God!

Second Sunday after Epiphany
Ordinary Time 2

Isaiah 49:1–7

Psalm 40:1–11

1 Corinthians 1:1–9

John 1:29–42

In Preparation for Worship

Lamb of God,
Holy Dove,
refresh us with your Spirit,
immerse us in your love.

Call to Worship

Do not conceal or keep to yourselves
what you know of the mercies of the Lord.
> Tell the glad news of deliverance.
> Tell of God's faithfulness to the great congregation!

Happy are the humble who make the Lord their trust.
Happy are those who wait patiently for the Lord.
> Surely our cause is with you, O Lord.
> Nothing and no one can compare with you.

If I were to tell of God's wondrous deeds
they could never be counted!

Let us sing a new song to the Lord,
a song of praise to our incomparable God.

Opening Prayer

Mighty God, even when it seems we have labored in vain and spent all our energy for nothing, you remain our strength. Surely our reward is with you. We gather as those who share in Christ's mission. As he is our light, so let him shine through us, that all the world might know your truth and salvation.

Call to Confession

The word of the Lord is a sharp sword, capable of cutting with directness and power. God's truth lays to waste all falsehood and pretension, exposes what is harmful and deadly, and makes room for the growth of what is healthful, fruitful, and good. Let us submit our hearts to God's merciful examination in the light of truth.

Prayer of Confession

O Lord our God, we confess that we live amidst many false gods; moreover, in moments of doubt, pride, rebellion, and disobedience, we have thoughtlessly turned to them and away from you. Our iniquities often overtake us, O God, until we cannot see and our hearts fail us. Do not withhold your mercy, O Lord, but draw us up from the pit of desolation. Let your steadfast love and faithfulness keep us safe forever!

Declaration of Forgiveness

The Lord has heard your cries, O people. God has set your feet upon the rock of Christ Jesus and will surely guide your steps securely along the tried, the true, the ancient Way. Now treasure this word of Christ Jesus, your saving help, within your heart. For he is the Lamb who takes away the sin of the world; thus, he has taken away your sin. Truly, in Jesus Christ, you are forgiven!

Presentation of Tithes and Offerings

You who have been enriched in speech and knowledge; you who are not lacking in any spiritual gift; you who enjoy the fellowship of Christ, who strengthens you to the end: know that your cause is with the Lord! Therefore, let your whole heart, your whole mind, your whole strength, all your devotion, and a portion of your provisions be spent in service to God, in whom we have an eternal reward.

Prayer of Dedication

Be glorified, O God, you who require no sacrifice. For we have nothing to sacrifice that is not already yours, but we delight to do your will, and we desire to have your word on our lips, your love in our hearts. May your Spirit descend upon us once again, and upon these offerings dedicated to your name, that in their distribution you would be exalted.

The Blessing

In the Spirit, you are baptized with fire;
in Christ, a light to the nations.
Therefore, go forth in joy, in peace,
and in the strength of the Lord,
to share the gospel with those
whom God will call through you.

Third Sunday after Epiphany
Ordinary Time 3

Isaiah 9:1–4

Psalm 27:1, 4–9

1 Corinthians 1:10–18

Matthew 4:12–23

In Preparation for Worship

O Lord, you are our light and our salvation,
our rock, our stronghold, our strength.
Grant us sanctuary in your holy temple, and shelter us,
whether the day brings trouble or tranquility,
that we might behold your beauty,
and seek your face in wonder.

Call to Worship

Rejoice before the Lord as with joy at the harvest.
Exult before the Lord in the fullness of God's presence!
>**You, O God, have greatly added to your people.**
>**You, O Lord, have increased our joy!**

Sing and make melody to the Lord our God.
Fill the house of the Lord with shouts of jubilation!
>**For the Lord has gathered us under the folds of his tent.**
>**The house of God is opened to those who seek him.**

I ask only to dwell with the LORD forever,
to behold the beauty of the face of the LORD.
> **Come, my heart says, seek the face of God.**
> **Your face, O LORD, do I seek!**

Opening Prayer

Healing God, we long for you in whom we know unity and harmony; we seek you from whom we have grace and love. Grant us the same mind that was in Christ Jesus; inspire us with the knowledge of your gracious will; and teach us the wisdom—the redeeming wisdom—of the power of the cross.

Call to Confession

Jesus came preaching repentance and the kingdom of heaven. At the same time, he came healing every disease. The One who insists we redirect our lives toward the kingdom is the very One who offers us shelter, who sets us high on a rock, who is, indeed, our stronghold. Everything required for the sinner's salvation has been provided by the One who is our salvation. Thus, we have every reason to have confidence in Christ as we confess our sin.

Prayer of Confession

O God our salvation, hear our confession. We have too often taken the cross of Christ for granted, or regarded it, in our foolishness, as though the cross were emptied of its power. Moreover, we have created and exacerbated rifts and divisions in the body of Christ, your church. Hear our confession, O God, and forgive us, for you have always been our help. Do not cast us off or forsake us, O God of our salvation, but restore true peace to your people, those united in gratitude for the saving power of our crucified Lord, Jesus Christ, in whose name we pray.

Declaration of Forgiveness

There will be no gloom, but glory for those once in anguish, those held in contempt, those on whom the light of Christ has dawned. For Christ has broken the rod of the oppressor, having taken the yoke of the burden of sin upon his own shoulders. The Son of God has borne the chastisement for us. The cross of Christ is the power of God on our behalf. Therefore, do not neglect so great a salvation. By the grace of Jesus Christ, you are forgiven.

Presentation of Tithes and Offerings

What one thing do you ask of the Lord? What one thing would you seek above all else? Surely the Lord withholds no good thing from those who receive the Son, who desire the Spirit of God, who seek the face of the Lord. Let us then, likewise, render our gifts to God with gratitude, generosity, and joy.

Prayer of Dedication

Receive, O God, these tokens of devotion, offered with our joy and glad adoration. Use them, we pray, to draw into your kingdom those whom you call to be one with us in Christ, who is all in all.

The Blessing

Seek the Lord and inquire of the Spirit.
Abide in Christ and the power of the cross.
Proclaim the good news of the kingdom of God,
as you fish for new followers of Jesus.

Fourth Sunday after Epiphany
Ordinary Time 4

Micah 6:1–8

Psalm 15

1 Corinthians 1:18–31

Matthew 5:1–12

In Preparation for Worship

O Lord, we pray, speak your blessings into being;
Christ Jesus, impart your compassion and truth;
Holy Spirit, grant your wisdom to the lowly;
For you have been faithful to us from our youth!

Call to Worship

Come, all who would do what is right;
Come, all who would speak truth from the heart.
> **Let us gather in God's holy temple.**

Take up no reproach against your neighbor.
Make peace and honor those who fear the Lord!
> **God is faithful and steadfast and good!**
> **Let us remember the saving acts of the Lord!**

Indeed, God has told you what is good.
And what does the Lord require of you?
> **To do justice and love kindness and walk humbly with God.**
> **Let us, one and all, devote ourselves to such things!**

Opening Prayer

You have declared what is blessed, O God, and proclaimed that our joy is to be found in your kingdom! You have honored in your realm what the world despises: weakness, poverty, mourning, mercy, pity, meekness, purity, peace. Reveal yourself to us now, we pray, that we might know how you value even our frailties and love us even in our pain. Answer us, O God of majesty, Lord of mercy, that we might give you glory and praise!

Call to Confession

Let no one boast in the presence of God. For God has seen fit to shame the wise, the powerful, and the noble, by calling the simple, the weak, and the humble, by choosing what is low and despised in the world, things that are not, to reduce to nothing things that are. Therefore, we humbly approach the source of our life, confess our sin, and profess Christ as our sure and only hope of salvation.

Prayer of Confession

We have not known you through worldly wisdom, and we cannot grasp you with human strength. We can only recognize you as you reveal yourself, O God, yet we demure from your silent, watchful presence, for we know that you have seen and heard us at our worst, and we tremble to consider what our forgiveness has cost you. Confound our pretensions to wisdom, O Lord; confront our illusions with the message of your cross, that we might see in the crucified One, the true glory of loyalty and wisdom, the obedient perfection of humility and strength.

Declaration of Forgiveness

Christ Jesus is indeed the source of new life! He has become for us wisdom from God! The saving power of the message of the cross is that the divine-human person, Christ Jesus himself, is our righteousness, our sanctification, our redemption. Thanks be to God for this amazing gift of eternal life in Christ.

Presentation of Tithes and Offerings

The Lord does not require burnt offerings, as of old, but only that we would do justice by sharing, and love kindness by acting with humble generosity. With such gifts let us exalt the Lord Most High!

Prayer of Dedication

We thank you, O God, that you do not weary us, but set us free; that you do not condemn us, but you reveal to us all the mighty and wonderful deeds you have done to rescue us from death and to redeem us from sin. Though we are lowly, allow us to ascend and render to you these humble gifts, that you might use them in accordance with your wisdom for the salvation and freedom of others, in Jesus' name.

The Blessing

Blessed are you who belong to the Christ,
in whom your thirst for righteousness is satisfied.
Blessed are you who belong to heaven,
where God is worshipped in spirit and in truth.
Blessed are you who,
by the Holy Spirit and the love of peace,
are called children of God.
Go, rejoice, serve and be glad,
for though the world may scorn the cross,
your reward is great in heaven!

Fifth Sunday after Epiphany
Ordinary Time 5

Isaiah 58:1–9a (9b–12)

Psalm 112:1–9 (10)

1 Corinthians 2:1–12 (13–16)

Matthew 5:13–20

IN PREPARATION FOR WORSHIP

Surrounded by forces that defy your will,
we flee to you, O Giver of life.
For you have sent Jesus to fulfill
what we cannot. Alleluia! Alleluia!

CALL TO WORSHIP

What no eye has seen, what no ear has heard,
what God has prepared for those who love him—
> **these things are revealed to us through the Holy Spirit!**

Who has known the mind of the Lord, so as to instruct him?
For the Lord is not subject to the limits of human wisdom.
> **Fill us, O Spirit, and give us discernment.**
> **Grant each of us the mind of Christ.**

The Spirit searches everything, even the depths of God.
Therefore, illumine us, O Light of the world!
> **Keep covenant with us,**
> **that we may be salt and light for the world.**

Opening Prayer

O Lord our God, you have called us together to glorify you and declare your worth, to praise you and keep this day holy, to magnify your mighty name through tender acts of lovingkindness. Receive our worship, that the world may know, through the manifestations of your grace among us, that Jesus Christ is Lord!

Call to Confession [Isaiah 58 (select verses)]

The voice of the prophet:
"Announce to my people their rebellion,
to the house of Jacob their sins.
Yet day after day they seek me
and delight to know my ways,
as if they were a nation that practiced righteousness
and did not forsake the ordinance of their God; . . .
Such fasting as you do today will not make your voice heard on high. . . .
Is not this the fast that I choose: to loose the bonds of injustice,
to undo the thongs of the yoke, to let the oppressed go free,
and to break every yoke?
Is it not to share your bread with the hungry,
and bring the homeless poor into your house;
when you see the naked, to cover them,
and not to hide yourself from your own kin?
Then your light shall break forth like the dawn,
and your healing shall spring up quickly;
your vindicator shall go before you,
the glory of the Lord shall be your rear guard.
Then you shall call, and the Lord will answer;
you shall cry for help, and he will say, Here I am. . . .
Then your light shall rise in the darkness
and your gloom be like the noonday."

Prayer of Confession

Lord of the Sabbath, we confess we have often served our own interests when we should be serving you. We have rarely desisted from pursuing

our worldly goals; we have not loosed the bonds of injustice for others or broken the yokes of the oppressed. We have wearied ourselves, tried your unending patience, and allowed injustice to go unchecked; we stand exhausted and convicted. How desperately in need of your commanded rest are we and the whole of your creation! Forgive our sin, and our foolishness for being so long in asking; teach us the way to your restorative kingdom of truth, equity, mercy, and peace, for the sake of your name.

Declaration of Forgiveness

Happy are those who fear the LORD, who greatly delight in his commandments and in him who has fulfilled the commandments: Christ Jesus, who was crucified to set us free. Those who trust in him shall rise in the darkness as a light for others; they shall be upright and blessed, gracious, merciful, and righteous, and their righteousness will endure forever. Praise the LORD!

Presentation of Tithes and Offerings

It is well with those who deal generously and lend, who conduct their affairs with justice. For the righteous will never be moved; they will be remembered forever. Let us offer our tithes and gifts to the LORD.

Prayer of Dedication

Holy One, in Christ you have not given us the spirit of the world, but your Holy Spirit, that we may understand the gifts you have bestowed on us. Grant us now such understanding, that as you bless and direct our use of these gifts, we might delight in the glory of your grace at work in our midst, in Jesus' name.

The Blessing

You are the salt of the earth.
You are the light of the world.
For your faith rests not on human wisdom, but on the power of God.

Therefore, let your light shine before others,
so that they may see your good works
and give glory to your Father in heaven!

Sixth Sunday after Epiphany / Proper 1
Ordinary Time 6

Deuteronomy 30:15–20

Psalm 119:1–8

1 Corinthians 3:1–9

Matthew 5:21–37

IN PREPARATION FOR WORSHIP

Eternal God,
fill us with your Spirit of Truth,
that we might praise and give you glory
with upright and undivided hearts,
in the name of the single-minded Reconciler.

CALL TO WORSHIP [Psalm 119:1–8]

Happy are those whose way is blameless,
who walk in the law of the LORD.
> **Happy are those who keep his decrees,**
> **who seek him with their whole heart,**
> **who also do no wrong, but walk in his ways.**

You have commanded your precepts to be kept diligently.
O that my ways may be steadfast in keeping your statutes!
> **Then I shall not be put to shame,**
> **having my eyes fixed on all your commandments.**

I will praise you with an upright heart,
when I learn your righteous ordinances.
> **I will observe your statutes;**
> **do not utterly forsake me.**

or [see Deuteronomy 30:15–20]

The God of the covenant has set before us
either life and prosperity, or death and adversity.
> **We choose life, so that we, and our children, may live long**
> **in the blessed provision of the Lord our God.**

Therefore, worship the Lord your God; obey and hold fast to him.
> **For in the Lord we have life and length of days.**

Opening Prayer

Holy God, you have set before us two ways: one that leads to life and prosperity, another that leads to death and adversity. Draw near, we pray, and speak to us of your commandments; give us a pure heart and a willing spirit to obey you in accordance with your rule of love, as we learn to walk in your ways and continue in your Word. Bless us, O Lord, that we might become more numerous and live long in the land you have given us. Make our hearts faithful and true in every way that we might never turn away, never fail to hear or heed you, and never be led astray to bow down to other gods and serve them. Give us courage and inspiration, faith and hope, so that we might choose life and hold fast to you in loving obedience all of our days.

Call to Confession

Truly we should speak and live as spiritual people, but far too often we live as people of the flesh, as no more than infants in Christ. For as long as there is jealousy and quarreling among the people of God, are we not of the flesh, behaving according to human inclinations? As Jesus has taught us, whatever causes us to sin is to be cut off and thrown away; for it is better to lose a part of one's body than for the whole body to go to destruction. Let us confess our sins.

Prayer of Confession

Merciful God, we confess we have been quick to judge others in anger, but slow to judge ourselves by the same standards; we have received forgiveness, but denied it to others; we have broken your commandments, if not by outright disobedience, then by failing to keep them in our hearts; and we have allowed the flesh to resist and rebel against your Spirit. Forgive our sins, O Lord, and bless us with the freedom that is ours when we do the work of forgiveness well. Refresh us with the joy of your Spirit, that we might be led and inspired by the breezes that flow from your gracious presence, from the ancient gardens to the eternal mansions; in the name of Christ we pray.

Declaration of Forgiveness

All of us have a common purpose in Christ, yet each of us will receive wages according to our labors. For we are God's servants, working together in worship and mission. Therefore, let us be reconciled to one another in accordance with the atonement of Jesus Christ, by whose sacrifice we have been reconciled to God. Truly, in Jesus Christ, you are forgiven; therefore, be at peace with God, with one another, and with yourself.

Presentation of Tithes and Offerings

The Lord of the covenant promises happiness and prosperity when his people seek him and observe his commandments, not as a means of self-justification, but as the journey of discovery and delight in his ways. Let us therefore plant our seeds and water them, that God may give them growth to the delight of all and for the glory of his name.

Prayer of Dedication

What joy it is, O God, to be united in Christ in your common purpose; what a delight to participate in your fruitful ways! Though our part is small and our gifts are humble, you are able to unite and grow them and bring about a new and glorious result. Do so, we pray, with this offering, in the name of Jesus.

The Blessing

May the Word of God take deep root in your hearts,
that the good fruit of your life and labor may reflect
the purity of your love for Christ,
for his whole church,
and for the world to whom you are sent in the Spirit
as upright ambassadors of the family of God.

Seventh Sunday after Epiphany / Proper 2
Ordinary Time 7

Leviticus 19:1–2, 9–18

Psalm 119:33–40

1 Corinthians 3:10–11, 16–23

Matthew 5:38–48

IN PREPARATION FOR WORSHIP

We approach you, O God, far short of your perfection;
confident of your love, yet limited in our vision.
Turn our hearts to your Spirit, our eyes to your light,
our ears to your Word, our wills to your ways,
that we may be ever more like you
and, like you, ever more
faithful and loyal, holy and true.

CALL TO WORSHIP

You shall be holy, says the LORD,
for I the LORD your God am holy.
> **Teach me, O LORD, the way of your statutes,**
> **and I will observe it to the end.**

You shall leave the gleanings for the poor and the alien:
I am the LORD your God.
> **Turn my heart to your decrees, O LORD,**
> **and not to selfish gain.**

You shall not hate in your heart anyone of your kin.
You shall reprove your neighbor or incur guilt yourself.
You shall not bear a grudge against any of your people,
but you shall love your neighbor as yourself: I am the Lord.
> Give us understanding, discernment, strength, and love,
> that we may keep your law and observe it wholeheartedly.
> For we are gathered to worship you, O Lord,
> to hear and receive your Living Word.

Opening Prayer

Eternal God, your glory far exceeds what we are able to perceive, yet your Word declares that we are your temple and your Spirit dwells within us. How can we comprehend your steadfast love and your humble grace in coming down to meet us? How can we thank you for entrusting us fully to your Son Jesus Christ, the heir of all things, with whom we stand to inherit your kingdom? Surely we can never fully survey the ground of your grace! Yet receive our devotion, adoration, and gratitude, and draw ever nearer for our instruction and sanctification, that we might bear the light of your truth and the joy of your Spirit, and live for the praise of your glory.

Call to Confession

Jesus said, be perfect, as your heavenly Father is perfect; love your enemies and pray for those who persecute you. Such a standard is far beyond our human capacity for love and perfection, but with God all things are possible. Therefore, let us confess how far we have fallen through sin, and profess our need for and our confidence in Christ, in whom we are truly reconciled to God and set free for the life of faith.

Prayer of Confession

Holy and gracious God, we confess that we are prone to shifting from the sure foundation of Christ to the unstable sands of the world; we often build ourselves up with pretense and possessions that will not withstand the test of time, much less the spiritual test of your Spirit and your Word. Turn our eyes, we pray, from looking at vanities; turn our hearts to serve you alone. Forgive us, and turn away the disgrace that we dread; give us life in your ways, for truly your ordinances are good, and in the righteousness of Jesus Christ you give us all things needful for life on earth and life in heaven.

Declaration of Forgiveness

The unlimited love to which God would have us aspire is the same love with which he has enfolded us into Christ. There is nothing lacking: nothing the world can add to God's wisdom, nothing our love can add to God's love. For no one can build a foundation other than the one that has been laid; that foundation is Jesus Christ. Let us not be deceived. If we think we are wise in this age, we should become fools in order to become wise. For the wisdom of this world is foolishness with God. But the grace and mercy of God and the blood of Jesus Christ have the power to redeem, and the gospel of forgiveness is the power of salvation. Friends, I declare to you, in the name of Jesus Christ, we are forgiven. Alleluia! Amen.

Presentation of Tithes and Offerings

Sharing with the poor is holy to the Lord. The restraint with which the people of God reap only what is needed and leave provision for those who have little distinguishes us from the world and our God from the idols of the nations. Let us turn our hearts to the just decrees of our holy God, for in Christ all things are ours, and let us act counter to the selfishness of the world, that we might bless those in need.

Prayer of Dedication

According to your grace, O God, we have these gifts to share, and though they may seem large in our eyes, we know they are but a fraction of all that you have given us in Christ Jesus. Bless these provisions, therefore, that by the power of your Holy Spirit they might be put to holy use, by your holy people, and thus magnify your holy name.

The Blessing

You are God's temple and God's Spirit dwells in you.
All things are yours, as you belong to Christ.
Therefore, go in the name of the Lord Jesus Christ,
blessing whom you meet and showing them God's love.

Eighth Sunday after Epiphany / Proper 3
Ordinary Time 8

Isaiah 49:8–16a

Psalm 131

1 Corinthians 4:1–5

Matthew 6:24–34

In Preparation for Worship

From mountain roads and highways,
from far away and near,
we come to you who cannot forget us,
who has promised never to forsake us,
whose compassion for us exceeds even that
of our mothers who bore us.
Look to your hands, merciful Lord,
and remember, for there you have said
we are inscribed.

Call to Worship [Psalm 131]

O Lord, my heart is not lifted up,
my eyes are not raised too high;
> I do not occupy myself with things
> too great and too marvelous for me.

But I have calmed and quieted my soul,

like a weaned child with its mother;
> **my soul is like the weaned child that is with me.**

O Israel, hope in the Lord
> **from this time on and forevermore.**

or [Isaiah 49:13, 8b–10]

Sing for joy, O heavens, and exult, O earth!
Break forth, O mountains, into singing!
> **For the Lord has comforted his people,**
>> **and will have compassion on those who suffer distress.**

I have kept you and given you
as a covenant to the people,
> **saying to the prisoners, "Come out,"**
> **to those who are in darkness, "Show yourselves."**

They shall feed along the ways,
on all the bare heights shall be their pasture;
> **they shall neither hunger nor thirst,**
> **neither scorching wind nor sun shall strike them down,**

for he who has pity on them will lead them,
> **and by springs of water will guide them.**

Opening Prayer

Loving God, you are faithful and trustworthy in all things. You are our hope forever! Lead us, we pray, into your holy presence, that our souls might be calm, quiet, and grounded in your endless and merciful care, for our joy and your glory.

Call to Confession [see 1 Corinthians 4:1–5]

As servants of Christ and stewards of God's mysteries, it is expected that we will be found trustworthy. Although it matters little how others judge us, we are not acquitted by virtue of our indifference, excuses, or attempts at self-justification. It is the Lord alone who judges, it is the Lord alone who acquits, atones, and forgives. Therefore, do not pronounce judgment before the time, before the Lord comes, who will bring to light the things

Eighth Sunday after Epiphany / Proper 3—Ordinary Time 8

now hidden in darkness and will disclose the purposes of the heart. Let us confess our sins.

Prayer of Confession

Holy God, we confess we are an anxious people, overly concerned for ourselves, doubtful of our worth in your eyes. We try to prove ourselves in costly ways. Forgive us this failure of faith, and give us courage to trust that, as you have in your love deemed us worth dying for, there can be no greater proof of your love than your Son, Jesus Christ our Lord, for whom we thank you, and in whose name we pray.

Declaration of Forgiveness

Thus says the Lord: In a time of favor I have answered you, on a day of salvation I have helped you. No amount of worry can add a single hour to your life; but your Creator and Redeemer is also your Provider who values and cares for the lowliest creature. How much more, then, shall we be assured of this good news: in Christ Jesus, God has given us all that is needful for our salvation and peace. Therefore, be at peace, knowing that in Jesus Christ you are well and truly forgiven, and free to live the life of faith.

Presentation of Tithes and Offerings

No one can serve two masters; for a slave will either hate the one and love the other, or be devoted to the one and despise the other. We cannot serve both God and wealth. Therefore, as servants of Christ and stewards of God's mysteries, let us be trustworthy and free from worry, that we might seek the kingdom of God and his righteousness above all other things, and act upon the generous purposes of God that we treasure in our hearts.

Prayer of Dedication

Heavenly Father, what glory you show through your simple creatures! As you feed the birds of the air from your plentiful creation, as you nurture the lilies with water, soil, and sun, so we know that you care for us, and we trust in you wholeheartedly who are most to be trusted. Receive, therefore, what infidelity and anxiety would have us hoard, and reveal your righteous kingdom, glistering in our midst, wherein all of our needs are met in abundance.

The Blessing

Do not worry about your life, about what you will eat or drink or wear.
But consider the lilies of the field, how your heavenly Father clothes them;
and the birds of the air, how your heavenly Father feeds them.
Surely he will provide far more for you!
But strive first for the kingdom of God and his righteousness,
and all these things will be given to you as well.

Last Sunday after Epiphany
(Transfiguration Sunday)

Exodus 24:12–18
Psalm 2 OR 99
2 Peter 1:16–21
Matthew 17:1–9

In Preparation for Worship

We would see your glory, as a lamp shining in the darkness.
We would behold your majesty, as a new day dawns in the heart.
We would hear your voice, as the sound of rumbling thunder.
Let your face shine on us, O Lord! Let your sovereign Word be heard!

Call to Worship

Gather, O people, at the mountain of the Lord.
May the glory of the Lord be upon you!
> **Let clouds assemble around the throne of God.**
> **Let us attend to the Living Word!**

God himself has testified of Jesus:
"This is my Son, the Beloved One,
with whom I am well pleased! Listen to him!"
> **Let us take refuge in the Lord our God.**
> **Let us serve him with fear and reverent love.**

The prophecies are confirmed in Jesus Christ.

The law is fulfilled in Christ our Lord.
> **Transfigure and reform us, Lord,**
> **that we might reflect your image.**

Opening Prayer

Sovereign God, you are holy. King of Righteousness, you are true. May the praises of all your servants, whether in heaven above or on the earth below, highly exalt your majesty. Yet, as all creation tells of your greatness, we are bold to ask, O Lord: descend to us, abide with us, that we may perceive the light of your glory!

Call to Confession

Our God is a mighty King, a lover of justice, who establishes equity, who executes justice and righteousness among his people. The Lord is a forgiving God. Happy are all who take refuge in him. Let us approach our holy, forgiving God, confessing our sins, that we might be forgiven and renewed, refreshed and reformed, in accordance with the mission of Christ Jesus, the Beloved Son of God.

Prayer of Confession

God of Mercy, you are a forgiving God, and we are a people in need of forgiveness. You gave us the law to guide us, yet we have strayed from your paths. You commissioned the prophets to call us back, yet we have continued in our errant ways. Finally, you sent your Beloved Son, and commanded us to listen. Forgive us for every sin and every failure to hear and obey; renew us, reform us, and redress us, that we may show forth true faith and love in Christ.

Declaration of Forgiveness

The good news is fully confirmed by the Holy Spirit who inspired the prophets and the apostles. It is confirmed by the testimony of our heavenly Father, and by Christ Jesus himself, whose labors took him to a cross in Jerusalem, where he made the perfect priestly intercession on behalf of sinners. Therefore, let us attend to him at all times, as to a lamp shining in the darkness, for it is through Christ Jesus, the Living Word of God, that we have assurance of peace with God and guidance for our journey to the kingdom of heaven. Be assured and give thanks for this good news: in Jesus Christ we are forgiven.

Presentation of Tithes and Offerings

Having heard the prophetic message, let us honor God as the Spirit leads us, giving thanks for the past and the future coming of our Lord Jesus Christ, to which our worship, our witness, and our gifts shall testify.

Prayer of Dedication

Holy God, Majestic Glory, we have heard your voice and we ourselves can testify as eyewitnesses to your transforming grace in our lives. Sanctify these gifts, that they might seal and confirm our witness to your redeeming power in Jesus Christ, your crucified and risen Son.

The Blessing

The glory of the Lord is a devouring fire,
but his Word and Spirit he has given to you,
that you might tell the good news,
once hidden, now revealed,
that Jesus Christ is the Beloved of God,
and all creation shall soon acknowledge him.
Go in the strength of this Word,
and may the Spirit sustain you
with the divine presence
and the glorious vision of Christ.

Part II

The Paschal Cycle
Lent—Easter—Pentecost

Ash Wednesday (ABC)

Joel 2:1-2, 12-17 OR Isaiah 58:1-12
Psalm 51:1-17
2 Corinthians 5:20b—6:10
Matthew 6:1-6, 16-21

IN PREPARATION FOR WORSHIP
Our heavenly Father,
show me how you see me,
whether in a pallid or a pleasant light,
and let me not concern myself
with the esteem, the opinions, or the judgments of others.
For you alone know me fully, and doubtless
better than I know myself.

CALL TO WORSHIP [Joel 2:1-2, 15-16; Isaiah 58:3, 6, 8]
Let all the inhabitants of the land tremble,
for the day of the LORD is coming, it is near—
> **a day of darkness and gloom,**
> **a day of clouds and thick darkness!**

Sanctify a fast; call a solemn assembly;
gather the people; sanctify the congregation.
> "Why do we fast, but you do not see?
> **Why humble ourselves, but you do not notice?"**

Thus says the LORD: "Is not this the fast that I choose:

to loose the bonds of injustice, to let the oppressed go free?
> "Then your light shall break forth like the dawn,
> and your healing shall spring up quickly."
> Let us return to the Lord with all our hearts.

Opening Prayer

O Lord, you know our inner thoughts and all that weighs upon each heart. Yet, how we long to voice our laments to you, to express our grief and sadness at all that is corrupt in the world, in this nation, in the church, in our communities, in our relationships, and in ourselves. We are especially grieved at our failure, as your people, to faithfully live according to your ways, and to show the world your righteousness in our lives. But spare your people, O Lord, and do not allow others to stumble because of our sin; let us not become a byword, for then the nations might say, "Where is their God?" Rather, sanctify your people, that your name may be known, proclaimed, and honored, not only among us, but to the ends of the earth.

Call to Confession [Isaiah 58:9–10; Joel 2:13]

As the prophets have said: If you remove the yoke from among you, the pointing of the finger and the speaking of evil; if you offer your food to the hungry and satisfy the needs of the afflicted, then your light shall rise in the darkness and your gloom be like the noonday. Return, therefore, to the Lord, your God, for he is gracious and merciful, slow to anger, and abounding in steadfast love. Let us confess our sin in penitence and faith.

Prayer of Confession [Psalm 51]

Have mercy on me, O God,
according to your steadfast love;
> according to your abundant mercy
> blot out my transgressions.
Wash me thoroughly from my iniquity,
> and cleanse me from my sin.
For I know my transgressions,

and my sin is ever before me.
Against you, you alone, have I sinned,
> and done what is evil in your sight,
so that you are justified in your sentence
> and blameless when you pass judgment.
Indeed, I was born guilty,
> a sinner when my mother conceived me.
You desire truth in the inward being;
> therefore teach me wisdom in my secret heart.
Purge me with hyssop, and I shall be clean;
> wash me, and I shall be whiter than snow.
Let me hear joy and gladness;
> let the bones that you have crushed rejoice.
Hide your face from my sins,
> and blot out all my iniquities.
Create in me a clean heart, O God,
> and put a new and right spirit within me.
Do not cast me away from your presence,
> and do not take your Holy Spirit from me.
Restore to me the joy of your salvation,
> and sustain in me a willing spirit.
Then I will teach transgressors your ways,
> and sinners will return to you.
Deliver me from bloodshed, O God,
O God of my salvation,
> and my tongue will sing aloud of your deliverance.
O Lord, open my lips,
> and my mouth will declare your praise.
For you have no delight in sacrifice;
> if I were to give a burnt offering, you would not be pleased.
The sacrifice acceptable to God is a broken spirit;
> a broken and contrite heart, O God, you will not despise.

OR

Righteous God, we confess that though we ask of you righteous judgments, we have allowed violence and oppression to fill our streets and destroy the land, quarreling to divide your church, and self-interest to consume our time and your resources. We show outward signs of dismay, but have failed to rectify injustice with mercy or to nurture the inward disposition from which such righteousness and compassion spring. Forgive us, O Lord, and inspire us to generous acts of sharing, stewardship, and goodness. Go behind and before us, as both our vindicator and rear guard; make us once more like a well-watered garden and rebuild the ancient, ruined foundations; be for us the restorer of our streets, that the world may witness your presence among us, and say, "We too shall have the Lord as our God!"

Declaration of Forgiveness

"See, now is the acceptable time; see, now is the day of salvation!" Only do not accept the grace of God in vain; but know that for our sake God made Jesus Christ to be sin who knew no sin, so that in Christ we might become the righteousness of God. Having been thus reconciled to God, we are now ambassadors for Christ, as God is making his appeal through us. Therefore, working together with him, let us entreat others on behalf of Christ, putting no obstacle in anyone's way, but announcing God's grace and mercy, through Jesus Christ, in every circumstance: "At an acceptable time I have listened to you, and on a day of salvation I have helped you." Thanks be God!

Presentation of Tithes and Offerings [Matthew 6:2–4, 19–21]

Jesus said, "Whenever you give alms, do not sound a trumpet before you, as the hypocrites do in the synagogues and in the streets, so that they may be praised by others. Truly I tell you, they have received their reward. But when you give alms, do not let your left hand know what your right hand is doing, so that your alms may be done in secret; and your Father who sees in secret will reward you. . . . Do not store up for yourselves treasures on earth, where moth and rust consume and where thieves break in and steal; but store up . . . treasures in heaven, where neither moth nor rust consumes and where thieves do not break in and steal. For where your treasure is, there your heart will be also." Let us offer our alms and gifts in accordance with the teaching of Christ.

PRAYER OF DEDICATION

Direct, O God, what we offer you this day to those for whom it might bring the greatest joy, serve the greatest need, and through whom it would give you the greatest glory. Give us endurance and resolution in our giving, that we might be true in our hearts and faithful in our actions; as those who are poor, yet making many rich; as those having nothing, and yet possessing everything.

THE BLESSING [Isaiah 58:11]

The LORD guide you continually, strengthen you,
and satisfy your needs in all the parched places,
that you may be like a well-watered garden,
like a spring whose waters never fail.

First Sunday in Lent

Genesis 2:15–17; 3:1–7
Psalm 32
Romans 5:12–19
Matthew 4:1–11

In Preparation for Worship

We have had enough, O God, of the false promises of this world.
We hunger for the truth of your everlasting Word.
Even if we must endure deprivation,
inspire us and lead us to eternal salvation.

Call to Worship

Do not fail to acknowledge your sins.
Harbor no deceit within.
> **You, O God, see through our disguises.**
> **Have mercy upon us and set our hearts upright.**

Do not keep silent or waste away with groaning.
Direct your heartfelt prayers to the Lord.
> **You, O God, are a shelter for your people.**
> **Preserve us from trouble and cover our sins.**

Do not be stubborn or without understanding.
Listen and savor the word of the Lord.
> **You, O God, forgive our transgressions.**
> **Teach us your ways and lead us in truth.**

Opening Prayer

Merciful God, in giving the free gift of Jesus Christ to the world, you have set aside condemnation, so that your grace might direct our discipleship and guide us to our eternal home. Come to us, we pray, and strengthen our faith for the journey that lies before us, that your righteousness may sustain us through this and every season of testing, and that, as we learn to resist worldly temptations and distractions, we might exercise obedience and know the joy of it in Christ.

Call to Confession

Just as sin came into the world through one human being, and death came through sin, so much more abundantly has the grace of God come into the world through one human being, Jesus Christ, whose power is greater than that of sin, and who has authority to justify and transform sinners through the free gift of God's righteousness. Let us confess our sins to the One who willingly exercises his power for the sake of those who do not hide from God, but rather take refuge in him.

Prayer of Confession

Living God, we cry to you for mercy and forgiveness, for only you can take away our sin. We confess we have known too much evil and failed to faithfully choose the good. We have turned from your Word, put you to the test, and allowed other gods to exploit us, stealing our time, our resources, our affection, and our attention. Forgive us, O God, for we long to be restored in our fellowship with you, to have faith enough to rely on you for everything, and to stand in the grace by which you make us righteous through the free gift of your beloved Son Jesus Christ, in whose name we pray.

Declaration of Forgiveness

Happy are those whose transgression is forgiven, whose sin is covered. Happy are those to whom the Lord imputes no iniquity, in whose spirit there is no deceit, for the Lord forgives the guilt of those who confess their sin. Indeed, through the one man, Jesus Christ, and through his freely obedient act of righteousness, you are forgiven, justified, and able to stand in the grace of God. Therefore, rejoice and be at peace.

Presentation of Tithes and Offerings

God provides both for our earthly needs and for our eternal life and joy and blessedness. Meanwhile, each day affords the opportunity to show kindness to our neighbors and to share with others the abundance of grace that we have received. In light of eternity and the grace of heaven, let us be free with our earthly gifts.

Prayer of Dedication

O Lord, you alone are worthy of our worship and devotion; you alone are able to sustain us with the true bread of heaven. Therefore, we present these earthly elements, and with them we offer you our lives of service, which you have purchased through the obedience of Christ. Direct our stewardship, we pray. Guide us by your Holy Spirit, as we seek to administer these gifts in a manner that is pleasing to you.

The Blessing

May the steadfast love of the LORD surround you.
May the Holy Spirit of truth uphold you.
May the grace and goodness of our Lord Jesus Christ
keep your hearts upright and make you glad as you trust
and follow him in the everlasting way.

Second Sunday in Lent

Genesis 12:1–4a
Psalm 121
Romans 4:1–5, 13–17
John 3:1–17

IN PREPARATION FOR WORSHIP
Thank you, O God, for the gift of life.
Now give us new life in your Spirit.
Reveal and open your kingdom, we pray,
and give us the faith to receive it.

CALL TO WORSHIP
The LORD has promised to make a great nation
of those who believe his promises.
> Come, O LORD! For you give life to the dead.
> You bring into being those things that were not!
The LORD reckons faith as righteousness
to those who, like Abraham, trust in him.
> Come, O LORD! You are worthy to be praised.
> For your promises rest on your grace alone.
The children of faith shall inherit the earth.
Such is the trustworthy promise of God.
> Come, O LORD! You are worthy of trust.
> May our worship declare your glory!

Opening Prayer

God of Majesty, you are our maker, our protector, our provider. You shield us from the scorching sun; you shelter us from the evil one; you keep vigilant watch over all our comings and goings. Therefore, we lift our eyes to you; we place our trust in you, for you are our help and our eternal salvation, through Jesus Christ our Lord.

Call to Confession

On what basis do we approach God to confess our sin? Not on the basis of the law! For the law brings wrath. Rather, we confess to God on the basis of faith. For the Lord promised Abraham that he would inherit the land, and Abraham believed God and his faith was counted as righteousness; such faith is sufficient ground on which to approach our Holy God with humility, yet with confidence; for repentance from sin is faith toward God. With no works about which we may boast before God, we can nevertheless trust him who justifies the ungodly to forgive our ungodly thoughts, words, and deeds.

Prayer of Confession

Almighty God, truly your Son has come, ushering in your kingdom and performing mighty deeds in your presence. Yet, we confess, we have been slow of heart to believe; we have remained attached to worldly concerns and neglected spiritual matters of eternal importance. Forgive us, O Lord, for wasting so much time and attention on things that will not endure and that do not satisfy. Refresh us and give us new life under the grace and in the power of your Holy Spirit. Give us the resolve to do your will, the wisdom to discern your truth, and the living water of your Spirit, that we may drink deeply and forever find refreshment in the river of life; through Christ Jesus our Lord.

Declaration of Forgiveness

Friends, hear and believe the good news: "Just as Moses lifted up the serpent in the wilderness, so must the Son of Man be lifted up, that whoever believes in him may have eternal life. For God so loved the world that he gave his only Son, so that everyone who believes in him may not perish but may have eternal life. Indeed, God did not send the Son into the world to condemn the world, but in order that the world might be saved through him." Therefore, the promise of life depends on faith in Jesus Christ, in order that the promise may rest on grace and be guaranteed to all who have faith in the presence of God, who gives life to the dead and calls into existence the things that do not exist. Know that in Christ you are forgiven and be at peace. Thanks be to God!

Presentation of Tithes and Offerings

Any temporal gifts that we might offer to God are not to be compared with the eternal and unfading inheritance we have in Christ through faith. Therefore, let us with thanksgiving devote our best gifts to God, who ever keeps watch over the faithful and provides for those who trust in him.

Prayer of Dedication

Eternal God, the gift of your Son for our salvation far exceeds the riches of the wealthy or what the most diligent laborer could earn. Yet, you willingly receive such humble gifts as we can give. Use these offerings, we pray, for the ongoing mission of your church, and for the reconciling ministry of your Son, that in their use your gospel might reach those who have not yet received the gift of faith, for your joy and for their salvation, through Jesus Christ our Lord.

The Blessing

May the Spirit of the Living God give you new life and peace, in the presence of God, through the faith of Jesus Christ, the author of life and giver of salvation.

Third Sunday in Lent

Exodus 17:1–7
Psalm 95
Romans 5:1–11
John 4:5–42

IN PREPARATION FOR WORSHIP

Through all our troubles, help us to endure,
and fashion endurance into character.
Prove our character, that we might hope
with a hope that will neither doubt nor waver.
All this we know you are sure to do,
for you have filled us with love,
your love that is true.

CALL TO WORSHIP [see Psalm 95]

O come, let us sing to the Lord.
Let us make a joyful noise to the rock of our salvation!
> **For the Lord is a great God**
> **who reigns supreme over all other gods.**

O come, let us worship and bow down.
Let us kneel before the Lord, our Maker.
> **For the Lord is our God,**
> **and we are his people, the sheep of his pasture.**

O that today you would heed the voice of the Lord!

Do not harden your hearts as did the Israelites in the wilderness.
>   **For their generation did not regard the ways of the Lord,**
>   **and they did not enter the land of promise.**

Opening Prayer

All praise be to you, O God our Deliverer! We lift our hands to you, O Lord our Banner. For you bring forth water from desert rocks and provide relief from the enemy. Reveal yourself, O Holy One. Speak to us your words of life. Remind us of your mighty works and direct us to the works you would have us do. For we would worship you in spirit and in truth.

Call to Confession

Our gracious God did not wait for sinners to become righteous on their own, or for the weak to become strong in themselves, before he reconciled himself to sinful humanity. But at the right time, while we were still in our sins, Christ died for the ungodly. Who, then, is more trustworthy than God to hear our confession and to take away our sin? Who more than God, who has given us access to grace through the Lord Jesus Christ?

Prayer of Confession

Living God, we confess we often drink what does not quench our thirst and eat that which does not satisfy. We allow ourselves to be driven by foolish impulses and thoughtless cravings, and we forget your vital and lasting provisions: the living water of the Lord Jesus Christ, and the lasting food that comes of doing your will. Forgive our vain strivings, O God. Be present to us in all your fullness, that we might partake of your eternal word and be equipped, empowered, and inspired to proclaim to others your gracious gift of eternal life in Christ.

Declaration of Forgiveness [see Romans 5:8–10, 1–2]

Friends, hear the good news! God has proven his love for us in that, while we still were sinners, Christ died for us. Much more surely then, now that we have been justified by his blood, will we be saved through him from the wrath of God. For if, as enemies, we were reconciled to God through the death of his Son, how much more surely shall we be saved by his resurrection! Therefore, since we are justified by faith, we have peace with God through our Lord Jesus Christ, through whom we have obtained access to this grace in which we stand. Know that in Jesus Christ we are forgiven, and be at peace.

Presentation of Tithes and Offerings

In the presence of God, let us give thanks; let us make a joyful noise to the Lord with songs of praise! For the sea and the dry land, from the depths of the earth to the heights of the mountains—all things belong to God, for he made them; and his love he has poured into our hearts through the gift of the Holy Spirit. In that spirit, let us offer what we have received from the open, generous, and gracious hand of God.

Prayer of Dedication

God of the harvest, we have always thought of the harvest field as yielding food for us to eat; but to hear Jesus tell it, it is our labor in the fields that is the best food of all, when we reach out to others, according to your will, and share the truth about Jesus Christ with them. What is more, we have Jesus' testimony that the fields are ripening and they await your laborers. Send out your laborers, therefore, O God, and if we are those laborers, then so be it. Lead us and inspire us—our words, our will, and our work—that our labor may indeed conform to your will, and that these gifts might be used to bring in a bountiful yield.

The Blessing

The Lord is among you—let there be no doubt!—
to give what is needed where it is least expected.
Go, therefore, in the name of Jesus,
and offer to all the water of life!

Fourth Sunday in Lent

1 Samuel 16:1–13
Psalm 23
Ephesians 5:8–14
John 9:1–41

IN PREPARATION FOR WORSHIP

In you, O Lord, in you—
to be in you makes all the difference;
therefore, come and meet us here,
that we may ever be in you.

CALL TO WORSHIP

Come to Christ, O people. Come.
Gather in the presence of your Sovereign Lord.
> **Open our eyes, O Light of the world!**
> **For though we may walk through vales of darkness,**
> **we shall yet see the light of life.**
Come to Christ, O people. Come.
Let us worship and bow down before the Living God.
> **Fill us, O Spirit. Let us feed on your Word,**
> **and bear the fruit of the light that is good, right, and true.**

Opening Prayer

O Lord our Shepherd, who protects and provides for the sheep, in your wisdom you have commanded us to keep this holy day of rest and to find renewal in your presence. Receive our prayers of gratitude for nourishing us with both temporal and eternal food, for giving us what is needful for the growth and the strength of spirit, soul, and body. Receive as well our songs of adoration and praise, for through your Son Jesus Christ you have prepared a place in your household for each of your children, that we might not only gather in your presence at the beginning of each new week, but live in your house forevermore.

Call to Confession

The Lord does not see as mortals see; they look on the outward appearance, but the Lord looks on the heart. Let us, therefore, examine our hearts and offer them to the Lord for examination. We do this by confessing those sins of which we are ashamed and those fruitless works we have done, that the Lord our Shepherd, in his grace, might forgive us, restore our souls, anoint us with his Spirit, and lead us in his way of righteousness and peace.

Prayer of Confession

We confess, O God, that we are often blind to your ways, deaf to your voice, and indifferent to your will. We often fail to do the works to which you have called us. We walk as though we are stumbling in the dark, though your holy light streams all around us. Forgive us, O Lord, for every sin and failure, every fearful retreat, every stubborn rebellion. Give each of us a pure heart, a clean mind, and a willing spirit, that your works might be revealed in your church, as you intend, under the grace and authority of Jesus Christ our Lord.

Declaration of Forgiveness [see Ephesians 5:8–14]

Hear the good news: Once you were darkness, but now in the Lord you are light. Live as children of light—for the fruit of the light is found in all that is good and right and true. Everything exposed in the light of the Lord becomes visible, for everything that becomes visible is light. Therefore it says, "Sleeper, awake! Rise from the dead, and Christ will shine on you." Truly, as those who live and walk in the light of our gracious and merciful Lord, you are forgiven; therefore, be at peace.

Presentation of Tithes and Offerings

Friends, let us try to find out what is pleasing to the Lord. Let us search our hearts, as God does, and produce good fruit as befitting the children of light. Let us offer good and true gifts, that others might see in them the bounteous provision of the Lord our Shepherd.

Prayer of Dedication

O Lord, although in this world we hear many messages meant to stir up discontent, we need only think of you, and we soon recognize and rejoice that you have met our greatest needs; indeed, your provisions abound and your goodness and mercy attend us wherever we go. We thank you that, from our brimming cups, we have these gifts to share. May they be blessed as they pass from our hands to yours, and from yours to those whose eyes you would open in the light of your love, in Jesus Christ our Lord.

The Blessing

May the Shepherd lead and guide you;
may the Christ illumine and restore you;
may the Spirit comfort and bless you;
and may your works of love come to light
and be pleasing in the sight of our triune God!

Fifth Sunday in Lent

Ezekiel 37:1–14
Psalm 130
Romans 8:6–11
John 11:1–45

In Preparation for Worship

Lord God,
we remember your mighty word through your prophet
and your great victory in Jesus Christ;
now regard your servants and consider your church:
"Can these bones live?"
Surely, with your Spirit all things are possible.
Blow afresh, O Lord, and give life to your gathered people!

Call to Worship

The Lord said, "Prophesy to these bones, and say to them:
O dry bones, hear the word of the Lord:
> I will cause breath to enter you, and you shall live.
> I will lay sinews and cause flesh to come upon you,
> and cover you with skin, and put breath in you,
> and you shall live and know that I am the Lord."
Jesus said, "I am the resurrection and the life.
Those who believe in me, even though they die, will live,
and everyone who lives and believes in me will never die.

Do you believe this?"
>   **Truly, Jesus is the Christ, the Son of the Living God.**
>   **He, the crucified, lives again, and in Christ we too shall live.**
>   **Let us worship God!**

Opening Prayer

God of Glory, who sent Jesus Christ to raise the dead to life, you reveal your glory to those who believe in your Son, who trust he is the resurrection and the life. Reveal yourself to us in this place, that we may see the light of Christ in this world and walk without stumbling, living and serving you with the full assurance that we shall dwell with you in fellowship and joy for all eternity; this we ask in the name of Jesus Christ our Lord.

Call to Confession [Romans 8:6–9]

Listen to what the Spirit says to the church: To set the mind on the flesh is death, but to set the mind on the Spirit is life and peace. For the mind that is set on the flesh is hostile to God; it does not submit to God's law—indeed it cannot, and those who are in the flesh cannot please God. Anyone who does not have the Spirit of Christ does not belong to him. Let us confess our sins to God, renouncing the ways of the flesh and seeking new life in the Spirit, in accordance with the will of the one God who has the power to break the bonds of sin and death.

Prayer of Confession [Psalm 130]

Out of the depths I cry to you, O Lord.
>   **Lord, hear my voice!**

Let your ears be attentive to the voice of my supplications!
If you, O Lord, should mark iniquities,
>   **Lord, who could stand?**

But there is forgiveness with you,
>   **so that you may be revered.**

I wait for the Lord, my soul waits,
>   **and in his word I hope;**

my soul waits for the Lord

more than those who watch for the morning,
> more than those who watch for the morning.

O Israel, hope in the Lord!
> For with him there is steadfast love,

and with him is great power to redeem.
> It is he who will redeem Israel
> from all its iniquities.

or [see Ezekiel 37:11–14]

You, O Lord, have spoken, and we know that you will act according to your promise. Therefore, we are bold to approach you and confess that our sins are beyond our capacity to cure; they, like grave clothes, bind us so that we cannot free ourselves. But you, O Lord, have promised to bring your people up from the grave, to restore us to our heritage, and to make us stand upright. Moreover, you have promised to put your Spirit within us, and though our sins have grieved your Spirit, we have confidence that your gracious power is greater than the powers of sin and death. Fulfill your promise, Lord God of Israel. Forgive us, fill us, and restore us to new life; in Jesus' name.

Declaration of Forgiveness [Romans 8:9–11]

Hear the gospel of our Lord Jesus Christ: You are not in the flesh; you are in the Spirit, since the Spirit of God dwells in you. But if Christ is in you, though the body is dead because of sin, the Spirit is life because of righteousness. If the Spirit of him who raised Jesus from the dead dwells in you, he who raised Christ from the dead will give life to your mortal bodies also through his Spirit that dwells in you. Therefore, know that you are forgiven, free from all that has held you captive to sin, and able to walk in newness of life!

Presentation of Tithes and Offerings

The Lord Jesus, though able to defeat death with a word, did not withhold his tears at the death and the grief of his friends. Such is the grace of the one who comes all the way to the tomb to raise us up. Let us therefore offer our gifts to God, in compassion for the poor and the dispirited, that he might lift heavy hearts and encourage those in need. For if we believe in Jesus, we shall surely see the glory of God.

Prayer of Dedication

O God, you are glorified in so many ways, but never more wonderfully than when you take some small, lifeless token and make it live and breathe, flourish and sing. Toward that wonderful end, we offer these small gifts, that you might demonstrate your glory with them, and that we ourselves might live to glorify you anew, both this day and forever; in the name of him who is the resurrection and the life.

The Blessing

Set your mind on the Holy Spirit
for righteousness and life, for joy and peace;
and may the good news of Jesus Christ,
the resurrection and the life,
gladden your heart and revive your spirit,
that you may walk and work, worship and testify
to the glory of our triune God!

Sixth Sunday in Lent
(Palm Sunday)

Isaiah 50:4–9a
Psalm 118:1–2, 19–29
Philippians 2:5–11
Matthew 21:1–11

In Preparation for Worship

Morning by morning, day after day,
you awaken and give us life, O Lord.
Apportion your Word to your servants,
your children, that we may have
hope and strength, faith and courage, humility and love
according to the mind of Christ Jesus himself,
in whose name we pray.

Call to Worship [Psalm 118:1–2, 19–29]

O give thanks to the Lord, for he is good;
his steadfast love endures forever! Let Israel say,
> "His steadfast love endures forever."

Open to me the gates of righteousness,
that I may enter through them and give thanks to the Lord.
> This is the gate of the Lord;
> the righteous shall enter through it.

I thank you that you have answered me
and have become my salvation.
> The stone that the builders rejected has become the chief cornerstone.
> This is the LORD's doing; it is marvelous in our eyes.

This is the day that the LORD has made;
> let us rejoice and be glad in it.

Save us, we beseech you, O LORD!
> O LORD, we beseech you, give us success!

Blessed is the one who comes in the name of the LORD.
> We bless you from the house of the LORD.

The LORD is God, and he has given us light.
> Bind the festal procession with branches,
> up to the horns of the altar.

You are my God, and I will give thanks to you;
> you are my God, I will extol you.

O give thanks to the LORD, for he is good,
> for his steadfast love endures forever!

OR

Awaken, O people, and attend to the LORD.
May the Lord GOD open the ears of his people.
> Let us gather and listen for the Word that sustains us.
> Morning by morning, it is bread for the weary.

Do not turn back or be dismayed.
> For the one who vindicates our hope is near.

OPENING PRAYER

O Lord our GOD, truly you know how to sustain the weary with a word. Morning by morning you awaken us to listen as those who are taught. Open our ears, O LORD, and give us courage that we might not be daunted or turn away from you. For you alone offer sure redemption; with your help, we will not be disgraced. For our Lord Jesus Christ has gone this way before, having fixed his resolve, knowing the suffering that awaited him in Jerusalem. Make us ready, we pray, to worship and serve you with utmost devotion and faithfulness, in the name of Jesus, the name above all other names.

CALL TO CONFESSION [Philippians 2:5–8]

Let the same mind be in you that was in Christ Jesus, who, though he was in the form of God, did not regard equality with God as something to be exploited, but emptied himself, taking the form of a slave, being born in human likeness; and being found in human form, he humbled himself and became obedient to the point of death—even death on a cross. In the spirit of humility and obedience, let us confess our sins, the very sins for which Christ Jesus has died, knowing that this rejected one has become the very cornerstone of our faith.

PRAYER OF CONFESSION

Our Lord Jesus Christ, when you rode into Jerusalem upon a donkey's colt, you came in peace and humility, to shouts of "Hosanna! Save us!" Truly, you came to save us. Yet, such a salvation was not what we expected. We confess that we have wanted salvation on our own terms. Unwilling to humble ourselves, presuming to know better, we have repeatedly resisted your will and your call to repentance and faith. Forgive us, O Lord, for all the ways in which we have kept you at arm's length. We recognize now, more than ever, that we need your saving grace. We pray, once again, "Hosanna to the Son of David! Blessed is the One who comes in the name of the Lord! Hosanna in the highest heaven!"

DECLARATION OF FORGIVENESS [Isaiah 50:8–9; Philippians 2:9–11]

"Who will contend with me? Let us stand up together. Who are my adversaries? Let them confront me. It is the Lord God who helps me; who will declare me guilty?" Jesus Christ, the Son of God, in whom there is no sin and over whom sin has no power, has obediently suffered death for our sins. Therefore, God has highly exalted him and given him the name that is above every name, so that at the name of Jesus every knee should bend, in heaven and on earth and under the earth, and every tongue should confess that Jesus Christ is Lord, to the glory of God the Father. Know that, in Christ, we are forgiven and free to live for the praise of his glory. Thanks be to God!

Presentation of Tithes and Offerings

All things temporal wear out like a garment; the moth will eat them up. But the Lord works wonders and performs great marvels, even with what the world rejects. Therefore, while we have the time and the temporary custody of our earthly treasure, let us readily and humbly offer our gifts of thanks to God.

Prayer of Dedication

Holy God, your glory reaches to the highest heaven, and the name of your Son exceeds all other names. Surely, one day every knee shall bow and every tongue shall confess Jesus as Lord. In keeping with this inspired vision and the hope of the future glory, we offer these gifts; may they be used, as we would be used, to exalt and praise you, the one God: Father, Son, and Holy Spirit.

The Blessing

Let the same mind be in you that was in Christ Jesus,
the same humble, obedient spirit of grace and service.
Go with his mind; go in that spirit;
go in the blessed peace of the triune God,
that you may always be ready
to sustain the weary with the gospel word.

Sixth Sunday in Lent
(Passion Sunday)

Isaiah 50:4–9a
Psalm 31:9–16
Philippians 2:5–11
Matthew 26:14—27:66 or Matthew 27:11–54

In Preparation for Worship

Despite whatever scorn or humiliation
we face in this world, O Lord,
despite whatever shame,
we trust in you to deliver us,
you who bore the cross for us,
for such is your long-suffering nature,
and your faithful love for your children.

Call to Worship

With the tongue of a teacher and the ear of a listener,
he came in obedience and did not turn back.
> **He turned his cheek to those struck him,**
> **and offered his back to the scourge.**

He set his face, and was not rebellious;
none can find any fault with him.
> **Let us seek him, whose vindication has come:**
> **Jesus the Christ, the highly exalted One.**

Sixth Sunday in Lent (Passion Sunday) 97

OPENING PRAYER

Lord Jesus, though mocked and derided, you were not put to shame; though beaten and spat upon, you were not disgraced; though innocent and unjustly crucified, you, the Son of God, have been vindicated by your sinless life and exalted to the right hand of power. As we gather to remember your suffering, fill us with your Spirit, conform our thoughts to yours, and teach us your ways, that the world might see in your body, the church, your ongoing ministry of redeeming grace toward this fallen, spent, and weary world.

CALL TO CONFESSION

As members of the body of Christ, each one of us knows in some measure the suffering of Christ. But Jesus, who alone was completely innocent of transgression, has undergone great suffering on behalf of the whole world, conforming his human will to the will of the heavenly Father, and refusing to answer a single false charge against him. We, the recipients of his grace, are those to whom it falls to confess the need of the human race for his unmerited intercession, and our faith that he is indeed the loving redeemer, sent by God. In the name of Jesus, let us pray with the Spirit of Christ, singing in the psalms.

LITANY OF CONFESSION [Psalm 31:9–16]

Be gracious to me, O LORD, for I am in distress;
    my eye wastes away from grief,
    my soul and body also.
For my life is spent with sorrow,
and my years with sighing;
    my strength fails because of my misery,
    and my bones waste away.
I am the scorn of all my adversaries,
a horror to my neighbors,
    an object of dread to my acquaintances;
    those who see me in the street flee from me.
I have passed out of mind like one who is dead;
    I have become like a broken vessel.

For I hear the whispering of many—terror all around!—
as they scheme together against me,
> as they plot to take my life.
But I trust in you, O Lord;
> I say, "You are my God."
My times are in your hand;
> deliver me from the hand of my enemies and persecutors.
Let your face shine upon your servant;
> save me in your steadfast love.

Declaration of Forgiveness

Truly, no accuser of Christ shall find any ground on which to stand. No one can stand against him who has taken his stand for us, for the very sinners whom he came to redeem. Friends, hear the good news: It is the Lord God who helps us; who then will declare us guilty? Know that in Jesus Christ you are forgiven, and be at peace.

Presentation of Tithes and Offerings

There is no exploitation in the family, the household, or the economy of God. If Jesus, the Son of God, did not regard his equality with God as something to be exploited, surely our labors and our gifts find their proper expression in service—humble and willing, generous and cheerful service. Let us submit our offerings with the mind of Christ.

Prayer of Dedication

As you humbled and emptied yourself, Lord Jesus, so you established a pattern for our lives, a pattern of obedient, selfless service. As you were obedient even to the point of death on a cross, so we see that we should value nothing on this earth more than faithfulness to you, whose death leads to resurrection all who believe in you and promises a whole new creation. Bless these gifts, we pray, for the service and the glory of your kingdom, where you now reign with our heavenly Father and the Holy Spirit, one God both now and forever.

The Blessing

He emptied himself, taking the form of a slave:
Follow him, and offer like service.
He became obedient to the point of death:
Keep faith in him to your dying day.
God also highly exalted him;
so shall you be raised to new life and endowed
with the Spirit as you in turn exalt the Lord Jesus
and praise his glorious name.

Monday of Holy Week (ABC)

Isaiah 42:1–9
Psalm 36:5–11
Hebrews 9:11–15
John 12:1–11

In Preparation for Worship

Our wicks burn dimly, but you never grow faint.
Our bodies are bruised, but you are never crushed.
Neither will you quench or break those who seek you,
however weary we grow, however weak our faith.
Come then, O Light to the nations;
come and place your Spirit upon us.
For we await your teaching;
we long for nothing less.

Call to Worship [Isaiah 42:8–9]

The Lord God speaks, saying:
I am the Lord, that is my name;
> **my glory I give to no other,**
> **nor my praise to idols.**

See, the former things have come to pass,
and new things I now declare;
> **before they spring forth,**
> **I tell you of them.**

Let us seek the LORD who gives us his spirit.
Let us worship and praise the living God.

OPENING PRAYER [Psalm 36:7–9]

O God, through your steadfast love you invite all people to take refuge in the shadow of your wings, to feast on the abundance of your house, and to drink from the river of your delights. For with you is the fountain of life; in your light we see light. Illumine, therefore, your gathered people by the grace of your Holy Spirit, so that we may serve, in Jesus' name, as your guiding light to the nations.

CALL TO CONFESSION [Isaiah 42:1–4]

The LORD prefers to administer justice in gentleness. Speaking through the prophet, he testifies of the Messiah: I have put my spirit upon him to bring forth justice to the nations. He will not cry or lift up his voice, or make it heard in the street; a bruised reed he will not break, and a dimly burning wick he will not quench; he will faithfully bring forth justice. He will not grow faint or be crushed until he has established justice in the earth; and the coastlands wait for his teaching. With confidence in Christ's gentle compassion, and with respect for his insistence on the truth, let us confess our sins.

PRAYER OF CONFESSION [Psalm 36:5–6, 10]

We confess, O God, our devotion to you has been diminished by idolatry; our sense of your presence distracted by self-concern; our care for the poor diverted by arrogance; and our understanding of your righteous ways confused by the wickedness of the world. Forgive us, O Lord, for the sake of your steadfast love. For though your judgments are like the great deep, yet your faithfulness reaches to the clouds, and you save humans and animals alike, for such is your great compassion. Therefore, rectify our wayward hearts and show us your salvation in Jesus Christ our Lord.

Part II: The Paschal Cycle

Declaration of Forgiveness [Hebrews 9:11–12, 15]

Hear the good news: when Christ came as a high priest of the good things to come, he entered once for all into the Holy Place with his own blood, thus obtaining eternal redemption. For this reason he is the mediator of a new covenant, so that we who are called may receive the promised eternal inheritance, because a death has occurred that redeems us from our transgressions. Friends, the covenant and the promised inheritance are yours in Christ, in whom we have redemption, the forgiveness of our sins.

Presentation of Tithes and Offerings

Jesus said, "You always have the poor with you, but you do not always have me." Surely the poor are our perennial concern, yet only one thing will ensure that our concern is sincere, our compassion deep, our assistance generous, and our service in keeping with the redeeming mission of God, and that is our love for the Lord Jesus, in whose name and for whose glory we gratefully offer our gifts.

Prayer of Dedication [Isaiah 42:5–7]

O Lord God, who created the heavens and spread out the earth, who gives breath and spirit to all people: You have called us in righteousness, taken us by the hand, and kept us; in Christ, you have given us as a covenant to the people, a light to the nations, to open blind eyes and to release those who sit in darkness. Grant that these offerings may serve to shine your light abroad, to proclaim your victorious redemption in Christ, and to set free those who have been bound in chains of darkness and misery. Equip us to add our inspired testimony to the collective witness of your whole church through the ages, for your glory and in the name of Jesus Christ.

The Blessing

New things I now declare, says the Lord.
And I send you as a covenant to the people,
a light to the nations.
Therefore, may the Spirit of the Lord bless and keep you,
and may the Spirit of Christ lead you by the hand,

that you may be a blessed witness to those
with whom you have divine appointments,
those who await the teaching,
whose hearts the L ORD your God
is preparing, even now.

Tuesday of Holy Week (ABC)

Isaiah 49:1–7
Psalm 71:1–14
1 Corinthians 1:18–31
John 12:20–36

In Preparation for Worship

Father, glorify your name!
For when the hour had come for Jesus to suffer,
he asked you to do so.
And you said, with a voice like thunder,
"I have glorified it, and I will glorify it again."
This you promised for our sake and for generations
of those who would come to worship you
and to thank you for the gift of your Son,
whose prayer we offer anew:
Father, glorify your name!

Call to Worship [Isaiah 49:1, 3–4, 7]

Listen to me, O coastlands,
pay attention, you peoples from far away!
> The Lord called me before I was born;
> he said to me, "You are my servant,
> in whom I will be glorified."
But I said, "I have labored in vain,

I have spent my strength for nothing and vanity;
> yet surely my cause is with the Lord,
> and my reward with my God."

Thus says the Lord, the Redeemer of Israel and his Holy One,
to one deeply despised, abhorred by the nations, the slave of rulers:
> "Kings shall see and stand up, princes shall prostrate themselves,
> because of the Lord, who is faithful, the Holy One of Israel."

Opening Prayer

Holy One, you are the only wise God, and you are the source of our life in Christ Jesus, who has become for us wisdom and righteousness, sanctification and redemption. For though the message of the cross is foolishness to those who are perishing, it is to us the revelation of your saving power. Therefore, we gather to worship you, and to proclaim Jesus Christ, who, crucified for our sake, is the power and the wisdom of God. All glory and honor, all thanks and praise be to you, O God, Father, Son, and Holy Spirit, both now and forevermore.

Call to Confession

When Jesus speaks of the judgment of this world, he has the expulsion of the spiritual enemy in view. Furthermore, this very judgment, whereby the ruler of this world is driven out, coincides with the glory and exaltation of God. The same thing occurs in the confession of our sins: as we reject sin and renounce evil, the Lord is extolled and Christ is upheld as our Savior and Redeemer. Let us therefore glorify God in the confession and renunciation of our sins.

Prayer of Confession

In you, O Lord, we seek refuge; in your righteousness deliver and rescue your people; incline your ear and save us. For we confess that when the power of sin assaults our senses, we are often tempted; when it lies to us we are often lured; and we have yielded to it, to our shame. Forgive us for every wicked thought, every unjust deed, and every cruel word. Be

a rock of refuge, a strong fortress from the grasp of the enemy. For you are our hope and trust, O Lord, and our praise is continually of you.

Declaration of Forgiveness [1 Corinthians 1:21, 26–29]

Hear the good news: "Since, in the wisdom of God, the world did not know God through wisdom, God decided, through the foolishness of our proclamation, to save those who believe. For God's foolishness is wiser than human wisdom, and God's weakness is stronger than human strength. Consider your own call, brothers and sisters: not many of you were wise by human standards, not many were powerful, not many were of noble birth. But God chose what is foolish in the world to shame the wise; God chose what is weak in the world to shame the strong; God chose what is low and despised in the world, things that are not, to reduce to nothing things that are, so that no one might boast in the presence of God." Truly, friends, as those who are so foolish, weak, and lowly as to need the forgiveness and the grace of Jesus Christ, we may be assured that we are also chosen by God. Let us therefore praise and glorify the crucified Christ and our redeeming God! Thanks be to God!

Presentation of Tithes and Offerings [John 12:24, 26]

"Unless a grain of wheat falls to the earth and dies, it remains just a single grain; but if it dies, it bears much fruit." So said Jesus in reference to his own death. He also said, "Whoever serves me must follow me, and where I am, there will my servant be also." Let us make our offering an act of discipleship, following the example of Jesus in surrendering what we have held dear, that it may, apart from us and in the hands of the Lord, bear much fruit, for the glory of God.

Prayer of Dedication

You have said, O Lord, that you intend to gather all people to yourself and that your salvation shall reach to the end of the earth. We thank you that you have called us to share in your mission, that you give us strength and resources with which to do so. Receive and bless what we offer you this day, that your light and your summons may go forth from this place, in the name of Jesus, and that those whom you call may be restored to your covenant people, the great congregation of those you have redeemed.

The Blessing

May the light of Christ illumine you,
and the darkness not overtake you.
For in Christ you are the children of light,
a light to the nations,
lifting up the name of Jesus,
that Christ Jesus himself might draw all people
from the world of darkness into his marvelous kingdom of light.

Wednesday of Holy Week (ABC)

Isaiah 50:4–9a
Psalm 70
Hebrews 12:1–3
John 13:21–32

In Preparation for Worship

For the sake of the joy you endured the cross;
for the sake of the joy you disregarded its shame;
for the sake of the joy you have taken your seat
at the right hand of God,
where we look to you, Lord Jesus:
for the sake of the joy!

Call to Worship

Let all who seek the Lord rejoice and be glad.
> **Let us exult in the presence of God.**

Let those who love your salvation, O Lord,
say evermore, "God is great!"
> **Great, indeed, is our God,**
> **our help and our deliverer!**

The ears of the Lord are open
to the prayers of his people.
> **Come, let us offer our praise and petitions.**
> **Let us attend to the Word of the Lord.**

Opening Prayer

O Lord our God, what unwavering obedience, what enduring faith, what resolute perseverance you reveal to us in your Son Jesus Christ! He who was not dissuaded by hostility, who did not shrink from suffering, who brought faith to perfection—he has so much to teach us, and we have so much to learn. Awaken us, therefore, with your Word and sustain us with your Spirit, that we might learn such resolution and wisdom, and acquire such strength of faith as to give you glory and attain such joy as drew the Savior himself to your side in glory. This we ask in Jesus' name.

Call to Confession

There is no honor in accusation, but let all who seek the LORD confess their poverty before eternity and their need of grace. In confession, we set aside our burdens and the sin that clings so closely, that we might avail ourselves of the LORD's sure help and deliverance.

Prayer of Confession

O God, in the sight of heaven and before so many witnesses, we are surely poor and needy, for we can say nothing to conceal the sins we have committed, retract the hurtful words we have spoken, or erase our record of wrongs. Forgive us, O Lord, and hasten to our defense. For you alone, the only righteous judge, can silence the accuser. You, who alone are in a position to declare us guilty, are likewise alone in your sinless perfection. "He who vindicates me is near!" Therefore, if you forgive us, stand with us and advocate for us, no accuser remains who can speak without hypocrisy. O Lord, what marvelous grace you have shown us in Jesus Christ our Savior and Lord, in whose name we pray!

Declaration of Forgiveness

Friends in Christ, consider our Savior Jesus, who though he suffered such hostility from sinners, endured the cross and disregarded its shame for the sake of the joy that was set before him, the joy of vindicating God's judgment of sin and redeeming us from under sin's crushing weight. Therefore, do not grow weary or lose heart, for this same Jesus, the pioneer and perfecter of our faith, has taken his seat at the right hand of the throne of God, whence his gracious word will surely accord with his labors on earth to set us free. Believe the good news, and be at peace: in Jesus Christ we are forgiven.

Presentation of Tithes and Offerings

Our hope in God is never misplaced; neither is our confidence in Christ to do glorious things despite worldly opposition. Despite all appearances, heaven sees what is done on the earth, and no good deed done in the name of Jesus will be forgotten by God or fail to yield an eternal reward. Therefore, let us offer our gifts in faith, placing them in the hands of the One who gave them.

Prayer of Dedication

O God, you are great, and we rejoice in the salvation that you have given us in Jesus Christ. Indeed, you are glorified in him, and he in you, that all might know the truth of his testimony and the power of his cross to redeem. May these offerings witness to our faith in him, the One whose faith is perfect, the One whose faithful witness gives us inspiration to endure and persevere to the end; in Jesus' name we pray.

The Blessing

Set your sights on the joy of heaven,
on the fellowship of the saints,
and on the pioneer, Jesus Christ,
who has gone before you and awaits you,
and lines the road before you
with good works to do for his glory
and words of encouragement for the weary,
that they too might reach with you
the joy of heaven.

Maundy Thursday (ABC)

Exodus 12:1–4 (5–10) 11–14
Psalm 116:1–2, 12–19
1 Corinthians 11:23–26
John 13:1–17, 31b–35

In Preparation for Worship

You set us an example of humble service,
you, our Lord, wash our feet as a friend;
you command us anew to love one another
as you love us faithfully and truly to the end.

Call to Worship

Remember how the Son of Man was glorified:
> He said, "Little children,
> I am with you only a little longer."

Remember the example Jesus set for us:
> He said, "Very truly, I tell you,
> servants are not greater than their master.
> Nor are messengers greater than the one who sent them."

Remember how the Word made love the way:
> He said, "I give you a new commandment,
> that you love one another. Just as I have loved you,
> you should also love one another. By this everyone will know
> that you are my disciples, if you have love for one another."

Opening Prayer

You are the Lord, the God of our salvation! By the blood of the lamb at Passover, you saved your people Israel; by the cup of salvation, you have made with us a new covenant, sealed in the blood of your Son, Jesus Christ, the Holy Lamb of God, who takes away the sin of the world. How can we thank you for this most precious and priceless gift?

Call to Confession

We have a merciful and a gracious God who is willing to go to great lengths to free us from sin, and to liberate us from every form of enslavement. The Lord deems precious those who turn from sin in humility and simple faith, and Jesus Christ redeems all who trust in his saving death. Let us confess our sins and repent of them sincerely.

Prayer of Confession

We are not fully clean, O God, unless and until you cleanse us. We confess we can expect no share from you, O Christ, unless and until you wash us. We need you, Holy Spirit, to sanctify and protect us. Forgive and bless us, O God of Mercy, with strength to resist all evil and temptation; with the will to serve after your humble example; and with the strength to love one another and show forth your glory; in Jesus' name.

Declaration of Forgiveness

God has heard our supplications. The Lord has listened to our prayer. Jesus Christ is the answer to our need for forgiveness; he has died on the cross for our iniquities, his blood has been shed for the remission of our sins. Remember all that Jesus has done for you, and give thanks with your lives of loyalty and faith.

Presentation of Tithes and Offerings

Thanksgiving is the sacrifice that the LORD desires, hearts that recognize and requite God's love. As God's own people, let us lift up thankful hearts, offer gifts, and show gratitude to our saving Lord.

Prayer of Dedication

We owe you our lives; we owe our allegiance; thus, we offer you these provisions. You have led us even from death to life. Therefore, we trust you with all that we have; we invite you to mold us into all you would have us be. By our sacrifice of thanksgiving, may our loads be lightened for the journey of faith and our spirits set free to follow your leading, as you guide us into the paths of peace.

The Blessing

Serve one another, as God's blessing is upon you.
Strengthen one another, as the Spirit gives you hope.
Love one another, and the world shall know
that you belong to Christ, the Lord of love.

Good Friday (ABC)

Isaiah 52:12—53:12
Psalm 22
Hebrews 10:16-25 OR Hebrews 4:14-16; 5:7-9
John 18:1—19:42

IN PREPARATION FOR WORSHIP [see Isaiah 53:10-11]
Christ Jesus, suffering servant of God,
through your anguish you have made many righteous,
delivered many captives, revealed wondrous knowledge,
shed a great light, and made prosperous the will of the LORD.
May all here gathered make your life an offering for sin,
that, as we contemplate all you have done for us,
all vain, worldly powers will shut their mouths,
and we who revere you may become the righteous people
you are calling us to be.

CALL TO WORSHIP [Psalm 22:3-5, 23-24, 25-28]
You are holy, O LORD, enthroned on the praises of Israel.
> **In you our ancestors trusted;**
> **they trusted, and you delivered them.**
To you they cried, and were saved;
> **in you they trusted, and were not put to shame.**
You who fear the LORD, praise him!
All you offspring of Jacob, glorify him;

stand in awe of him, all you offspring of Israel!
> For he did not despise or abhor
> the affliction of the afflicted.

From you comes my praise in the great congregation.
> The poor shall eat and be satisfied;
> those who seek him shall praise the LORD.

May your hearts live forever!
All the ends of the earth shall remember and turn to the LORD;
> and all the families of the nations shall worship before him.
> For dominion belongs to the LORD, who rules over the nations.

OPENING PRAYER

O LORD God of Israel, for generations you have both gone before your people and been our rear guard; you have provided for us and defended us; you have taught us and reminded us of your mighty and astonishing deeds. Who could have imagined, O God, that the rejection and affliction of your Son Jesus Christ could become the basis of our hope and salvation? Yet this is what the prophets foretold and the apostles have confirmed; this is what your Word and Spirit have revealed. Grant us, therefore, the wisdom of your Spirit and the power of your holy presence, that we might better understand the mystery of redemption, glorify your name, and share the revelation of your love with those whom you are calling to yourself from the fruitless ways of this dying world.

CALL TO CONFESSION [Hebrews 10:19–23]

Surely, friends, we have confidence to enter the sanctuary by the blood of Jesus, by the new and living way he has opened for us through his flesh, and since we have a great priest over the household of God, let us approach with a true heart in full assurance of faith, with our hearts sprinkled clean from an evil conscience and our bodies washed with pure water. Let us hold fast to the confession of our hope without wavering, for he who has promised is faithful. With such confident hope in his cleansing grace, let us confess our sins.

or [Hebrews 4:14–16]

Since we have a great high priest who has passed through the heavens, Jesus, the Son of God, let us hold fast to our confession. For we do not have a high priest who is unable to sympathize with our weaknesses, but we have one who in every respect has been tested as we are, though he was without sin. Let us therefore approach the throne of grace with boldness, so that we may receive mercy and find grace to help in time of need.

Prayer of Confession [see Isaiah 53:4–6]

O Lord, holy and merciful, righteous and compassionate, we confess that we have all, like sheep, gone astray from your guidance; we have all turned to our own ways; we have rebelled against you and perverted justice, not only with our sin, but even despite our best intentions. Therefore, you sent your Son to suffer a perversion of justice for our sakes; you laid on him the iniquity of us all and afflicted him that he might bear our infirmities and carry our diseases. Wounded for our transgressions and crushed for our iniquities, he has borne the punishment that has made us whole, and by his bruises we are healed. In light of your farsighted provision, may the merciful intercession of Jesus heal us fully and impart your forgiveness. And what shall we say, in response to your grace, but thank you? What shall we do but bow before you and offer our lives in grateful service?

Declaration of Forgiveness [Hebrews 5:7–9; 10:16–17]

In the days of his flesh, Jesus offered up prayers and supplications, with loud cries and tears, to the one who was able to save him from death, and he was heard because of his reverent submission. Although he was a Son, he learned obedience through what he suffered; and having been made perfect, he became the source of eternal salvation for all who obey him. Thus, God has established a new covenant in Christ, saying, "I will put my laws in their hearts, and I will write them on their minds. I will remember their sins and their lawless deeds no more." Thanks be to God!

Presentation of Tithes and Offerings
[Hebrews 10:24; see also Isaiah 53:12]

Friends, in light of the great outpouring of Jesus on our behalf, let us consider how to provoke one another to love and good deeds, not neglecting to meet together, as is the habit of some, but encouraging one another, and all the more as we see the Day approaching. In a spirit of contrition, let us render unto God a sacrifice of thanksgiving, for the saving grace of Jesus Christ.

Prayer of Dedication

Eternal God, you foretold the exaltation of your servant Jesus Christ, and we would extol him and lift him up for the deep suffering he has undergone for our sake. Let our offering of thanks be a dividing of the spoil that your prophets envisioned, a proclamation of your accomplished redemption, a lauding of your holy name in the great congregation. Thanks be to God!

The Blessing

The Lord has delivered you from sin to salvation.
Christ Jesus has died that you might live.
Therefore, receive the fullness of his benefits,
that the news of his grace may be heard on your lips
by a world bereft of wisdom
and in need of renovation.

Easter *(The Resurrection of the Lord)*

Acts 10:34–43 OR Jeremiah 31:1–6
Psalm 118:1–2,14–24
Colossians 3:1–4 OR Acts 10:34–43
John 20:1–18 OR Matthew 28:1–10

In Preparation for Worship

Christ Jesus, you are our very life.
Our souls are hidden with you in God.
Therefore, we seek the things that are above,
forsaking the traps and temptations of this world.
We look to where you are seated, at God's right hand,
that we might know your will in all things
and, when you are revealed,
be revealed with you in glory.

Call to Worship

God loves us with an everlasting love.
God's faithfulness reaches beyond even the bounds of death!
> **Sing aloud the glad songs of victory!**
> **Tell of God's steadfast love!**

For Jesus Christ, the stone that the builders rejected,
has become the chief cornerstone,
the foundation of a whole new creation.
> **We shall not die, but we shall live**

Easter (The Resurrection of the Lord)

and recount the deeds of the Lord!
This is the gate of the Lord;
the righteous shall enter through it.
Come, let us worship the Lord our God!

Opening Prayer

Risen Savior, you are Lord of all! You are the one anointed with the Holy Spirit and with power to teach peace, to perform miraculous deeds, and to heal all who are oppressed. When the world rejected you and put you to death, you willingly suffered and died for the sake of righteousness. Now you are alive again, sovereign over all. You alone hold the keys to death. You alone give us hope for the future! We praise you, Lord Jesus! We adore you!

Call to Confession [Jeremiah 31:2–4]

Thus says the Lord: The people who survived the sword found grace in the wilderness; when Israel sought for rest, the Lord appeared from far away, saying: I have loved you with an everlasting love; therefore I have continued my faithfulness to you. Again I will build you, and you shall be built. Friends, with confidence in God's faithful love and his desire for our restoration, let us confess our sins.

Prayer of Confession

Lord of the Resurrection, we confess that we need your atoning sacrifice to cover our countless transgressions. You are both the judge who confronts us with the truth and the one who has paid the penalty for our sins. In rising from the dead, you escort us from the darkness of the tomb and usher us into the soft morning light, where our life is restored and we awaken to your grace. We believe in your goodwill; we trust in your good name. Forgive us, Lord, and lead us through this life of discipleship and into your realm of eternal life.

Declaration of Forgiveness [Acts 10:34–43]

Hear the gospel of our redemption: Jesus Christ is Lord of all! Anointed with the Holy Spirit and with power, he went about doing good and healing all who were oppressed by the devil. Though he was put to death, hanged on a tree, yet God raised him on the third day and allowed him to appear, not to all the people but to those who were chosen by God as witnesses, and who ate and drank with him after he rose from the dead. He is the one ordained by God as judge of the living and the dead. All the prophets testify about him that everyone who believes in him receives forgiveness of sins through his name. Friends, know that in Jesus Christ you are forgiven, and give thanks to God!

Presentation of Tithes and Offerings [Jeremiah 31:5]

Thus the Lord has promised: "Again you shall plant vineyards on the mountains; the planters shall plant, and shall enjoy the fruit." Let us offer our gifts to God as vines planted, as seeds sown, that God might make them bear good fruit.

Prayer of Dedication

Hear our glad songs of victory, O God; for your right hand has done valiantly; your right hand is exalted, where the risen Christ is seated in power. As you have gained the victory over death, so let our lives of worship, and all our gifts, be guided toward and serve your eternal kingdom and life in the resurrection; in Jesus' name.

The Blessing

The Lord has become our eternal salvation.
For Jesus Christ has been raised from the dead.
Go, therefore, in peace and great joy
and tell others of this good news;
and may the Spirit of Christ,
our hope and glory,
fill, attend, and inspire you forevermore.

Easter Evening (ABC)

Isaiah 25:6–9
Psalm 114
1 Corinthians 5:6b–8
Luke 24:13–49

IN PREPARATION FOR WORSHIP

Lord Jesus Christ, risen Son of God,
we know that when you come again
you will be seeking faith on earth.
But for today, for now, if we are in disbelief,
it is simply due to joy at the news,
joy that the good news can be this good.
Be patient with us, therefore,
and open our joyful, tearful, disbelieving eyes,
that we may see you and know:
you are risen, indeed!

CALL TO WORSHIP [see Psalm 114]

Tremble, O earth, at the presence of the LORD,
    at the presence of the God of Jacob.
For the seas and the rivers
flee at the sight of the holy One of Israel.
    The mountains and the hills skip like lambs
    at the coming of the LORD, our mighty deliverer,

who turns the rock into a pool of water,
> **the flint into a spring of water.**
> **Let us worship our saving God.**

Opening Prayer

Lord Jesus, truly you are the Messiah, the One who suffered crucifixion and death, as God deemed necessary, and then entered into glory. Though your path from death to life has shaken heaven and earth, and your resurrection transcends our human understanding, yet you come speaking peace to your people, reassuring us that your mission of redemption is proceeding as planned. Come, O Christ, and teach us more of what the Scriptures reveal about you, that we may rejoice in your presence and delight in your victory.

Call to Confession [1 Corinthians 5:6–8]

As a little yeast leavens the whole batch of dough, let us clean out the old yeast so that we may be made new. For Christ, our paschal lamb, has been sacrificed. Therefore, let us celebrate the festival, not with the old yeast of malice and evil, but with the unleavened bread of sincerity and truth. Let us confess our sins.

Prayer of Confession

Holy God, we confess that our fears and doubts have clouded our vision and made us slow of heart to believe all that you have disclosed in your Word. What once were mysteries have now been revealed in the resurrection of your Son Jesus Christ, in his victory over death, and in his presence with your church in the opening of the Scriptures and in the breaking of the bread. Yet our senses have grown dull, our understanding shallow, and our faith tepid because of the sin we see in the world and in ourselves. Forgive us, O Lord, and speak to us anew of all that you have accomplished and all that you have designed to do through Jesus Christ, that our cold, dry hearts may be ablaze with your Spirit, with the love of the truth, and with joy in your goodness.

Declaration of Forgiveness [see Isaiah 25:6–7]

The LORD of hosts has promised to remove the shroud cast over all peoples and the sheet spread over all nations; he will swallow up death forever, and in its place he will prepare a feast. Then the Lord GOD will wipe away the tears from all faces, and the disgrace of his people he will take away from all the earth, for the LORD has spoken. It will be said on that day, "Lo, this is our God; we have waited for him, so that he might save us. This is the LORD for whom we have waited; let us be glad and rejoice in his salvation."

Presentation of Tithes and Offerings

Truly, it is in the act of sharing, the sharing of the Word and the sharing at the table, that Christ is revealed as alive among us. Such sharing is at the heart of our faith, as it affords us the opportunity to convey and demonstrate the love of Christ to others. Let us, therefore, in keeping with our way of life, share our gifts with the body of Christ, in the name of Jesus and for the mission of God.

Prayer of Dedication

What glorious news is your gospel, O God: the presence of Jesus Christ in our midst, the burning of the Holy Spirit in our hearts, the promised redemption of our weary bodies. Bless these gifts in the service of your good news, that as we share them in joy, the news would indeed spread to every corner of the world, that Jesus Christ is risen from the dead and that we are his witnesses to the praise of his glory.

The Blessing

Go with hearts aflame in the Spirit.
Go with your spirits attuned to Christ.
Go with this powerful, wonderful news:
death is defeated, Christ Jesus is risen,
repentance and forgiveness of sins are to be proclaimed
to all nations in his name.
May the presence and peace of Christ
be with you always.

Second Sunday of Easter

Acts 2:14a, 22–32

Psalm 16

1 Peter 1:3–9

John 20:19–31

In Preparation for Worship [Psalm 16:7–9a, 11; Acts 2:28]

I bless the Lord who gives me counsel;
in the night also my heart instructs me.
I keep the Lord always before me;
because he is at my right hand, I shall not be moved.
Therefore my heart is glad, and my soul rejoices;
my body also rests secure.
For you show me the path of life;
you will make me full of gladness
with your presence.

Call to Worship [see Psalm 16:2–3; 1 Peter 1:7–8]

Say to the Lord, "You are my Lord;
I have no good apart from you."
> **Risen Lord, we have not seen you in the flesh;**
> **nevertheless, we know you live, and we believe in you!**

Take refuge in the Lord; rejoice in his presence.
Give glory to Jesus Christ, whom you have come to love.
> **Give us your Spirit to refine our faith;**

Second Sunday of Easter   125

teach us, O Christ, that our faith may prove true.
Thus says the Lord: "As for the holy ones in the land,
they are the noble, in whom is all my delight."
**All praise and glory and honor to Jesus Christ,
both now, here among us, and at his final coming.**

Opening Prayer

Almighty God, you have attested to your Son Jesus Christ through his wonderful signs and deeds of power, and with your definite plan and foreknowledge, he was handed over and crucified. But you, O God, have raised him up, having freed him from death; it was impossible for him to be held by the power of death, for he had not sinned and did not earn the wages of sin. Therefore, because you did not abandon him to the grave, and you did not allow his body to experience corruption, our hearts are glad and we rejoice, and we shall henceforth live in faith, for we who have been baptized into his body, now raised incorruptible from the dead, are born anew into this living hope of an undying inheritance, kept in heaven for your children. In such hope and in the name of Jesus Christ, we offer you our joyful adoration and praise!

Call to Confession

Even before the Pentecost, Jesus bestowed the Spirit upon his disciples with words of peace and with responsibility and authority either to forgive or to retain sins. Surely the broader witness of Scripture makes it clear that, while in some cases of church discipline, retention may be necessary for a time, thorough and complete forgiveness is the better way, just as we, in confession, express our hope that none of our own sins should be retained.

Prayer of Confession

Blessed and beloved God, we confess that we have not always been as free or thorough in forgiving others as we would have them be in forgiving us, yet, with your help, we would surrender any remaining grudges or vestiges of resentment at this time. We see every day corruption in

this world, as the power of death works on our mortal bodies, and we would know the good health that enjoys a clear conscience and exults in the freedom that is born of the sure hope of salvation. Forgive us, O Lord, of all our sins, our idolatrous acts and thoughtless oaths, and especially our slowness to believe and our slowness to forgive. As you did not allow your faithful Son Jesus Christ to remain in the tomb, so usher us from death to life, from sin to faith, from dark despair to radiant joy, that we might delight in your presence forevermore.

Declaration of Forgiveness [1 Peter 1:3–6, 9]

Blessed be the God and Father of our Lord Jesus Christ! By his great mercy he has given us a new birth into a living hope through the resurrection of Jesus Christ from the dead, and into an inheritance that is imperishable, undefiled, and unfading, kept in heaven for you, who are being protected by the power of God through faith for a salvation ready to be revealed in the last time. In this you rejoice, even if now for a little while you have had to suffer various trials, for you are receiving the outcome of your faith, the salvation of your souls. Thanks be to God!

Presentation of Tithes and Offerings

Our time in history notwithstanding, we are all witnesses to the resurrection of Jesus Christ. For we have heard and believed the testimony of the prophets and the apostles. Therefore, let our portion be to testify in our day, with our worship of our Lord and our God, and with gifts to be used for the blessing of others, that they too may come to believe and receive new life in Jesus Christ.

Prayer of Dedication

O Lord, you hold our lot; and you have appointed for your people a goodly heritage in Jesus Christ. Truly, having defeated death itself, you have apportioned life abundant for the fellowship of those who believe in your risen Son and confess him Lord of all. From your plenteous provisions, we offer these gifts in gratitude and faith, that you might use them as you continue your work in this world, drawing more and more people to faith in our Messiah, and that through faith in him they too may have life in the name of Jesus.

The Blessing

Receive the Holy Spirit, for you are sent in Jesus' name.
Honor the risen Christ with indescribable and glorious joy.
And may the power of God protect you,
keep your heavenly inheritance for you,
and unfold the plan of salvation before you
as you tell others of the good news of forgiveness
and the resurrection life.

Third Sunday of Easter

Acts 2:14a, 36–41
Psalm 116:1–4, 12–19
1 Peter 1:17–23
Luke 24:13–35

In Preparation for Worship

O God of the sacred journey,
open your Scriptures and lead us in,
open your kingdom, close at hand,
open our hearts to burn with love,
open our minds to understand,
open our eyes to recognize
your risen Son, our true companion.

Call to Worship

Set your faith and hope on God,
who has raised Jesus Christ from the dead!
> **Though we live as exiles,**
> **we praise our God who leads us home.**

In light of baptism and faith in the truth,
love one another deeply from the heart.
> **Though we have been slaves to sin,**
> **we worship Jesus Christ who has set us free to love.**

Truly, you have been born anew,
not of perishable but of imperishable seed.

Though we have been fearful and powerless,
we follow the Spirit who gives faith and power
to display God's reign upon the earth.
Let us worship our triune God.

OPENING PRAYER

We assemble in your sanctuary, O God our Creator, for in your holy presence many blessings abound. We gather in your name, O Christ our Redeemer, for in your company all bondage gives way to freedom. We meet in your presence, O Spirit of Truth, for in the warmth of your light we become the people you intend us to be in all your wisdom, beauty, grace, and love. Receive, therefore, our praise, adoration, and devotion, in Jesus' name.

CALL TO CONFESSION

God has made him both Lord and Messiah, this Jesus who was crucified. Therefore, let us repent, every one of us, in the name of Jesus Christ, so that our sins may be forgiven; and we shall be refreshed in the Holy Spirit. For the promise of forgiveness and eternal life is for us, for our children, and for all who are far away, everyone whom the Lord our God calls.

PRAYER OF CONFESSION

Holy Spirit of the Living God, we live among a corrupt generation. We cannot claim to be above it all, untouched by temptation and sin. For we too once rejected the crucified Christ, disobeyed his teaching, and followed our own ways. Nevertheless, you offer us salvation by the death of your precious Son. Therefore, we turn to you and invoke his name, Jesus, for you and your Son are faithful, merciful, loving, and kind; and we, forswearing our past sins, would be holy, even as you are holy!

DECLARATION OF FORGIVENESS

Hear anew the gospel of salvation: you have been ransomed from futility with the precious blood of Christ, like that of a lamb without defect or flaw. He was destined before the foundation of the world, and revealed at the end of the ages for your sake. Through him you have come to trust in God, who raised him from the dead and gave him glory, so that your faith and hope are set on God. Therefore, let us say with the psalmist, "I love the Lord, because he has heard my voice and my supplications. Because he inclined his ear to me, therefore I will call on him as long as I live." Let us also lift up the cup of salvation and call on the name of the Lord; let us pay our vows to the Lord in the presence of all his people. For he has loosed our bonds and set us free for eternal life and everlasting love. Thanks be to God!

Presentation of Tithes and Offerings

What shall we return to the Lord for all his bountiful gifts? Let us fulfill our vows to the Lord in the presence of all God's people; let us offer a sacrifice of thanksgiving and call on the name of the Lord.

Prayer of Dedication

O Lord, we are your servants, for with the precious blood of Christ Jesus our risen Lord, you have loosed the bonds of death. We revere and trust you, who destined Christ before the foundation of the world and revealed him at the end of the ages for the sake of your glory. Bless now these gifts, dedicated to his ongoing ministry, that the good news of the forgiveness of sins and the resurrection to eternal life may be made known to all nations, in Jesus' name.

The Blessing

The promise of God and the gift of the Holy Spirit are yours.
The sure and certain presence of the risen Lord Jesus is with you
in the fellowship of the faithful and in the breaking of the bread.
Therefore, knowing that you lack nothing for the journey,
go and make known all that the prophets have declared
concerning the Christ, our risen, ascended, and approaching King.

Fourth Sunday of Easter

Acts 2:42–47
Psalm 23
1 Peter 2:19–25
John 10:1–10

IN PREPARATION FOR WORSHIP

O Lord our Shepherd,
trustworthy guardian of our troubled souls,
sheep gate by which we enter your fold:
call us by name, and we will follow;
lead us to your verdant meadow;
quench our thirst with living water,
that we might dwell in your house forever!

CALL TO WORSHIP

Trust in the LORD. Listen for God.
Christ our Shepherd calls you by name.
>**Let us follow the voice of our guiding God,**
>**and hold fast to God's righteous way.**

Praise the LORD! Give thanks to God!
For you belong to the body of Christ.
>**Let us give thanks for salvation with generous hearts,**
>**and enjoy the fellowship of the family of God.**

Love the LORD! Draw near to God!

For Jesus has offered himself up for you.
> **Let us persevere in faith through this world of darkness,
> and know the glad freedom of the kingdom of God.**

Opening Prayer

Loving God, you are our shelter amidst the dangers of this world; you are our guide through the darkest valley; you are our comfort in times of distress; you are our provider despite all adversity. Therefore, we worship you, source of all goodness and mercy, in Jesus' name!

Call to Confession

The Lord, our Good Shepherd, is the restorer of the soul who leads us into what is right. Indeed, Christ is the gate by which the sheep enter God's fold. Jesus said, "I am the gate. Whoever enters by me will be saved, and will come in and go out and find pasture. The thief comes only to steal and kill and destroy. I came that they may have life, and have it abundantly." In humility and faith, let us confess our sin, our tendency to wander, our need for forgiveness, and our desire for the Lord's corrective guidance.

Prayer of Confession

God of mercy, in your Son Jesus Christ you have provided not only the needed atonement for sin, but also the marvelous prototype for life in your new creation; for when Jesus was abused he did not return abuse, and when he suffered he did not threaten. We confess we have not behaved with such grace, but by our stubbornness we have compounded suffering. Forgive us, heal us, and change our hearts, that we might share in the good work of shepherding the lost into the joy of salvation in Christ Jesus.

Declaration of Forgiveness

You have been called to endurance, because Christ has also suffered for you, leaving you an example, so that you should follow in his steps. "He committed no sin, and no deceit was found in his mouth." But he entrusted himself to the one who judges justly. He himself bore our sins in his body on the cross, so that, free from sins, we might live for righteousness; by his wounds you have been healed. For you were going astray like sheep, but now you have returned to the shepherd and guardian of your souls. Know that, in Jesus Christ, you are forgiven, and be at peace.

Presentation of Tithes and Offerings

As the early church freely shared their possessions, distributed the proceeds to those in need, and enjoyed the goodwill of all the people, let us likewise share our fellowship and our provisions with glad and generous hearts. Indeed, our sharing is an offering of praise to God.

Prayer of Dedication

Ever-faithful God, we remember and give thanks for your deeds of power, your signs and wonders, done for Israel of old and in your early church. We praise you that we, too, have known your presence and your gracious provision for us in Jesus Christ through the gift of your Spirit. Consecrate these gifts, we pray, as signs of the abundant life, that as you are glorified by their use, you might also add to our number those whom you have called to repentance, faith, and salvation, in the name of Jesus.

The Blessing

Fear no evil; but walk with the Lord.
Abide in the household of God forever,
and may the Holy Spirit of goodness and mercy,
faith and love, joy and gladness fill your hearts,
and bless you with the knowledge of Jesus Christ,
the shepherd and guardian of your souls.

Fifth Sunday of Easter

Acts 7:55–60
Psalm 31:1–5, 15–16
1 Peter 2:2–10
John 14:1–14

In Preparation for Worship

Loving God,
we have partaken of your blessings
and we know that you are good;
therefore, we seek your pure, spiritual food
that we might grow into maturity
as we rejoice in your salvation.

Call to Worship

Come to Christ, the living stone, rejected by mortals,
but chosen and precious in God's sight!
> **We believe in the Lord Jesus Christ!**
> **Therefore, we will not be put to shame!**

Let yourselves be built into a spiritual house,
for you are a royal priesthood!
> **We offer to God our praise and worship!**
> **We glorify the Lord by obedience and just living!**

Come to Christ, a precious, living stone,
for on this foundation you are a chosen race, a holy nation!

**God has dealt with us mercifully, who has called us
out of darkness and into his marvelous light!**

OPENING PRAYER

Faithful God, our times are in your hands. Let your face shine upon your servants here gathered; incline your ear and hear our prayer. Be for us a fortress of safety, a rock of refuge. Raise us up, as you did your servant Jesus. For we cannot save ourselves from death, but commit ourselves into your hands, O Lord, our faithful God.

CALL TO CONFESSION

The disobedient will stumble and fall; their feet will be caught in nets and snares. But God rescues, releases, liberates, and leads all who commit themselves to follow Christ Jesus and trust in his divine grace for freedom and salvation.

PRAYER OF CONFESSION

O God of our life, we cry to you for deliverance and forgiveness of our sins. Spirit of Truth, save us for the sake of your steadfast love; disabuse us of every lie and deception; protect us from all enemies that would lure us to destruction. O Christ our Way, do not retain our sins of the past; guard us in the present; and lead us along your sure path into our blessed future with you, into the joyous place that you are preparing for your people.

DECLARATION OF FORGIVENESS

Friends in Christ, hear this good news: Whoever believes in Christ will not be put to shame. For the One who stands at the right hand of God in glory—Jesus Christ, who is the Way, the Truth, and the Life—hears our prayers for forgiveness, authorizes us to forgive others, and has become the very way for us to be reconciled to God. Furthermore, he has promised to return for us that we might be together with the triune God in eternity. Forgiveness serves the ultimate will and purpose of God; therefore, be assured that in Jesus Christ we are indeed forgiven.

Presentation of Tithes and Offerings

As living stones in the spiritual house of God, as a holy people and participants in Christ's royal priesthood, let us offer spiritual sacrifices acceptable to God through Jesus Christ, in order that, through our giving and in all our living, we might proclaim the mighty acts of him who called us out of darkness into his marvelous light.

Prayer of Dedication

Holy God, by your grace and mercy, you have formed your people out of nothing; we who once were lost, and without hope in this world, are now a fellowship of love, founded on the faith of Jesus Christ, our precious head and cornerstone. Therefore, mindful of your mighty and merciful work on our behalf, we ask that you would bless and use these gifts to extend your grace and mercy to others, to call those who may yet be hopeless and lost in darkness, that the light of your gospel might reach them and draw them into the communion of those who love and believe in you, through Jesus Christ our Savior and Lord.

The Blessing

Do not let your hearts be troubled.
Believe in God; believe also in Jesus Christ the Son of God,
and receive anew the promised Holy Spirit.
For the one who believes in Jesus Christ
will also do the works of Christ, because God is One,
and whatever you ask in the name of Jesus
shall somehow be accomplished, for the glory of God!

Sixth Sunday of Easter

Acts 17:22–31
Psalm 66:8–20
1 Peter 3:13–22
John 14:15–21

IN PREPARATION FOR WORSHIP

Lord Jesus, you have said that the world
cannot receive your Holy Spirit,
for the world neither sees nor knows the Spirit of truth.
Yet this same Spirit abides with us and lives in us.
What a wonderful assurance this is,
for as we gather to worship you,
as we seek your presence and that of our heavenly Father,
we remember that we are not orphaned,
for by the gift of your Spirit,
you are already with us.

CALL TO WORSHIP

Christ has suffered once and for all,
the righteous for the unrighteous, in order to bring us to God.
> **In our hearts, therefore, let us sanctify Jesus Christ as Lord,**
> **who has saved us and delivered us through the waters of baptism.**

Do not be afraid, for we shall never be orphaned.
The Holy Spirit of truth and love is with us!

Let us tell what the Lord has done for us.
We are, in Christ, not driven by the flesh, but alive in the Spirit.
Cry aloud to God, that he may be extolled.
Let us declare the hope that is in us,
for we live and move and have our being in God!

Opening Prayer

We bless you, O God, for you have kept us among the living. Though you have tested us in many ways, you have brought us into your spacious, holy presence. Therefore, we worship you, and we will, with your help, fulfill the vows we have made to you. May the sound of our praises reach you, O Lord our God; this we ask in the name of Jesus Christ, who has ascended into heaven and is seated at your right hand, with angels, authorities, and powers made subject to him.

Call to Confession

Come and hear, all you who fear God, and consider what God does for those who cry out to him. If one cherishes iniquity in one's heart, the Lord will not listen. But if one appeals to God for a good conscience through the baptism of Christ, the Lord will hear and save, as he saved Noah and his family, and preserved them through the flood. God gives to all mortals life and breath and all things needful. Indeed God is not far from each one of us; he knows well our needs and desires that we should dwell with him in Jesus Christ his Son, through faith. In penitence and faith, let us confess our sin.

Prayer of Confession

O God our Creator, Lord of heaven and earth, you have commanded all people everywhere to repent, and you have fixed a day on which our Lord Jesus Christ will judge the world in righteousness. Yet we are far from able to pass the test, except by means of your gracious mercy and the forgiveness of our sins. Therefore, we appeal to you, through the resurrection of Jesus Christ: free us from all sin; grant each of us a clear conscience; raise your people into new life wherein your Holy Spirit empowers our good conduct and the exhibition of your reign among us.

Declaration of Forgiveness

Blessed be God, for he has not rejected our prayer or removed his steadfast love from us. But truly God has listened; he has given heed to the words of our prayer, and given assurance to all by raising from the dead our Lord Jesus Christ, who said, "Because I live, you also will live." Therefore, do not be afraid. Know that, in Jesus Christ, we are forgiven, and be at peace.

Presentation of Tithes and Offerings

Although the world does not see Jesus, the Son of God himself has promised that those who love him and keep his commandments are those to whom he will reveal himself. Surely, as the Spirit is seen by its influence on other things, like the wind moving in the grass and trees, so too Jesus is revealed among us as we bend to his will, as we walk according to the truth, as we honor his commandment to love. Let us lovingly give our gifts in Jesus' name.

Prayer of Dedication

Eternal God, Father, Son, and Holy Spirit, your love for us is clearly written in your Word and inscribed for all to see across the face of your whole creation. Therefore, we in turn profess and proclaim our love for you, and we seek to do so as you have commanded, by showing our love for one another in acts of service, in gifts of grace and gratitude, and in tender works of love. Bless these gifts, we pray, that they may be used wisely in your spirit of love, and that all who benefit from their use may know they are loved—loved by you and by those who love and believe in you.

The Blessing

People of God, be a people of praise.
Bless the God who has blessed you;
let the sound of his praise be heard wherever you go.

For the steadfast love of the L ORD is with you:
in the Spirit of Truth, in the returning Christ,
and in the heavenly Father, who—as one God—
has resolved to dwell with us eternally.
Such is the grace of this triune God
whom we love and serve.
Therefore, go in peace.

Ascension of the Lord (ABC)

Acts 1:1–11
Psalm 47 OR Psalm 93
Ephesians 1:15–23
Luke 24:44–53

IN PREPARATION FOR WORSHIP

As you ascended, Lord Jesus, you blessed your disciples;
and in that blessing they worshipped you in joy.
As we await your coming, let us also be so filled with joy
that our worship may testify to your presence,
yes, even in advance of your return.

CALL TO WORSHIP

Gather, O people, in the presence of the LORD.
Let a holy people assemble before the holy and everlasting God.
> **Even the floods exalt the LORD.**
> **The roaring sea glorifies him!**

Sing praises to our Sovereign God; sing praises!
God reigns over all the earth; sing praises with a psalm!
> **The LORD is awesome; he is highly exalted,**
> **the Most High over all the nations!**

Opening Prayer

Sovereign Christ, suffering did not silence your teaching; death could not extinguish your life. But you are demonstrably alive, governing your coming kingdom and sending your Spirit upon your church. Refresh us now, we pray, with the presence of your promised Spirit, that as we await your coming, we might fruitfully be about your work.

Call to Confession

Time and again, we concern ourselves with things beyond our knowledge and control; grasping for greater power and influence, we grow impatient and lose sight of God's purpose for our lives and Christ's mission through the church. Let us confess our sin.

Prayer of Confession

O Lord, your Word testifies that every prophecy concerning the Messiah must be fulfilled; but we have been slow to believe the Scriptures in their fullness, for they are daunting; and we have insinuated our selfish aims where we fail to understand your greater plan. Let us not remain blinded by sin, but forgive us, O God, and open our hearts to your gospel truth. Reveal yourself and teach us, that we may truly understand. Fix in our minds the marvelous news that forgiveness itself is your word to the nations, and by your grace we would serve the mission of your gospel, in Jesus' name.

Declaration of Forgiveness

You are Christ's witnesses; for as Jesus said to the early church, so he says to you: "See, I am sending upon you what my Father promised. By the gift of the Holy Spirit, you shall be clothed with power from on high. Forgiveness is to be proclaimed to all the nations." Thus, it is fitting that you who bear this good news should know for certain that in Jesus Christ you are forgiven. Thanks be to God, who has raised Jesus Christ from the dead, seated him far above every ruler and authority, and made him the head over all things for the church.

Presentation of Tithes and Offerings

God has chosen our heritage for us, and subdued the nations under the feet of Christ, who charges us to witness to the ends of the earth regarding the hope to which he has called us. Therefore, with lightness of heart, with the assurance of a glorious inheritance among the saints, and with faith in God's immeasurable greatness that is working on behalf of those who believe, let us offer our gifts.

Prayer of Dedication

We thank you, O Lord, that you have so established this world that it shall never be moved. Rather, you have moved the hearts of your people with faith in the Lord Jesus and with love toward all the saints; therefore, let these gifts be used in concert with the movement of your Spirit, in the service of your majesty, and in the blessing of those who stand in need.

The Blessing

As the Lord is robed, so be girded with strength.
As the Word is sure, so be filled with wisdom.
As the Spirit gives light, so receive the revelation
as you come to know him Who fills all in all.

Seventh Sunday of Easter

Acts 1:6–14
Psalm 68:1–10, 32–35
1 Peter 4:12–14; 5:6–11
John 17:1–11

In Preparation for Worship

O rider in the heavens, the ancient heavens:
send out your voice, your mighty voice.
For we, your people, are listening for your Word.

Call to Worship

Rejoice and be glad, for the risen Christ has ascended!
> **The Lord has ascended to God in glory!**
> **Jesus is one with our God in heaven.**

Sing to God, sing praises to his name;
raise a song to him who rides upon the clouds—
> **his name is the Lord—be exultant before him!**

Shout with joy for the glory of the Lord.
Give praise to the author of eternal life.
> **What is eternal life, but to know the one true God**
> **and Jesus Christ whom God has sent.**
> **Let us worship the God of glory!**

Opening Prayer

Blessed are you, holy God of glory, for you are awesome in your sanctuary! Great are you, O God of Israel, for you give power and strength to your people! May all who love and believe in you be one, even as you are one with Jesus Christ your Son, in perfect fellowship with your Holy Spirit. Empower us, we pray, to worship and serve you in the praise of your mighty name.

Call to Confession

Discipline yourselves, keep alert, and beware the devil who, like a roaring lion, is on the prowl, looking for someone to devour. Resist the tempter, and humble yourselves beneath the mighty hand of God. Cast all your cares on the Lord who cares for you; and the God of all grace, who has called you to his eternal glory in Christ, will himself restore, support, strengthen, and establish you. Let us confess our sins and our need of this gracious, redeeming God!

Prayer of Confession

We come to you, O God of light, forsaking the parched barrenness of our rebellious, undisciplined lives. We confess that our sins have cost you dearly, harmed our neighbors, and defiled your good creation. We languish and crave restoration. We have wandered and long to come home. We are desolate and need your grace. Forgive us, O Lord, and number us among the righteous, that we may be jubilant with joy in your holy service, for the sake of Jesus Christ our Lord.

Declaration of Forgiveness

Beloved, do not be surprised at the ordeals you face, as though something strange were happening to you, for everyone must be tested, and you know that believers everywhere are undergoing the same kinds of sufferings. But rejoice, give thanks, and remain steadfast in your faith, for in faith, Christ has overcome sin and temptation; in faith, Christ has overthrown death itself; in faith, Christ has defeated the devil; and in faith you who are in Christ share in his sufferings, as well as his victory, and the spirit of glory, which is the Spirit of God, rests upon you. Thanks be to God!

Presentation of Tithes and Offerings

"Father of orphans and protector of widows is God in his holy habitation. God gives the desolate a home to live in; he leads out the prisoners to prosperity." Let us offer our gifts with glad and generous hearts, for everything we have is from God.

Prayer of Dedication

O God, when you went out before your people and marched with them through the wilderness, the earth quaked, the heavens poured down rain at your presence. As we lift these offerings to you, send your blessings in abundance, O God; shower them abroad and restore your heritage. For you alone establish your people, and in your goodness, you provide for the needy.

The Blessing

The Son of God has authority over all people to give them eternal life. Go, therefore, in the name of Jesus, to glorify the ascended, sovereign Christ, that all might turn in their hearts to him,
for the life and the hope of which they stand in need.

Pentecost

Acts 2:1–21 OR Numbers 11:24–30
Psalm 104:24–34, 35b
1 Corinthians 12:3b–13 or Acts 2:1–21
John 20:19–23 OR John 7:37–39

In Preparation for Worship

We gather to await your promised coming,
eager to receive what you have to give.
Come, inspire, and make us ready,
Dove of fire, Spirit of love!

Litany for Pentecost

Holy Spirit of Creation,
in the beginning you moved across the face of the abyss;
you formed the heavens and the earth;
you made light shine out of darkness;
you gave order to the rhythms of night and day;
and you separated the waters from dry land.
> **Come, Holy Spirit!**

Holy Spirit of Life,
in the beginning you made seed-bearing plants to grow;
you filled the sky with birds and the seas with fish;
you covered the earth with animals of all sorts;
and you gave your breath to human beings.

Come, Holy Spirit!
Holy Spirit of Truth,
in ancient days you called into service
judges and priests, kings and prophets,
and you filled them with a passion for righteousness;
you ordered life in the law of Moses;
and in Jesus Christ, the Son of the Father,
you embodied the Truth for all creation.
Come, Holy Spirit!

[After a brief time of silent prayer, the leader continues.]

Holy Spirit of Prophecy,
you inspire the tongues of teachers and servants,
young and old, men and women,
with words that expose lies, injustice, oppression, and greed;
you fill their ears with your instruction,
their eyes with heavenly visions,
their minds with divine dreams.
Welcome, Holy Spirit!
Holy Spirit of Wisdom,
you write your Word on the hearts of your people;
you place your Word in the mouths of your messengers;
you bestow on your children marvelous gifts
and you direct us in their use.
Welcome, Holy Spirit!
Holy Spirit of Comfort,
you stir your people to compassion and mercy;
you heal the brokenhearted, give hope to the perishing,
and when life is gone, you raise the dead!
Welcome, Holy Spirit!
Forge anew your holy church!

CALL TO CONFESSION

The promises of God are such that no one can say, "Jesus is Lord," except by the Holy Spirit, but everyone who calls on the name of the Lord shall be saved. Let us, therefore, profess the saving Lordship of Jesus Christ, calling on his good name for salvation and asking forgiveness for all our sins.

Prayer of Confession

Gracious God, we confess that we allow our different gifts to divide rather than unite us. We are slow to discern your marvelous presence in one another, and quick to feel hurt when our gifts are not affirmed. Forgive us, O Lord, in your mercy. Set us free from selfishness and make us one in the body of Christ.

Declaration of Forgiveness

As the risen Christ repeatedly spoke peace to the disciples who abandoned him, so the risen Christ speaks peace today to those who hearts are troubled, whose consciences are burdened by guilt and sin. As the risen Christ showed his wounds to his disciples, so the risen Christ reminds us today that his suffering and death were undergone for our sake, to redemptive purpose, with resurrection in view. As the risen Christ breathed upon his disciples, thus imparting his Holy Spirit to them, sending them to share the good news, and charging them with the ministry of forgiveness, so the risen Christ offers us the living water of the Spirit, and sends us as bearers of his grace. Friends, know that in Christ you are forgiven; indeed, you are Christ's messengers of forgiveness and peace with God.

Presentation of Tithes and Offerings

The same Spirit gives a variety of gifts: wisdom, knowledge, faith, healing, miracles, prophecy, the discernment of spirits, tongues, and interpretation, and these gifts are to be shared for the good of all. Surely we are variously gifted, yet as we have been made to drink of the one Spirit, as we have all been baptized into the one body, let us share our gifts in the service of Christ, for we, though many, are all one in him.

Prayer of Dedication

O Lord, how manifold are your works! In wisdom you have made them all! When you give, we gather; when you open your hand, we are filled with good things. Send forth your Spirit, we pray, and use these gifts in your renewal of all things, that the earth itself and all the nations, your church and all whom you call to die and be reborn, may bless you and praise you in the power of the one Holy Spirit and in the name of Jesus Christ our Lord.

The Blessing

Sing to the Lord as long as you live;
sing praises to God while you have being.
Rejoice in the Spirit, that your thoughts and your words may please him,
and may Christ rejoice in his good works in you.

PART III

Ordinary Time (Propers 4–29)
Trinity—All Saints'—Christ the King

Trinity Sunday

Genesis 1:1–2:4a
Psalm 8
2 Corinthians 13:11–13
Matthew 28:16–20

In Preparation for Worship

Sovereign Lord, by whom all things were made;
Son of God, by whose cross was freedom won;
Holy Ghost, our closest friend,
our power and protector to the end:
you, the Trinity, are wholly One
in mind, in mission, in will, in being,
in word, in spirit, in everything!
May we abide forever in your holy peace,
in perfect unity and loving grace.

Call to Worship [see Psalm 8]

Your name, O Lord, is majestic. Your glory outshines the heavens. Yet you have placed all things under human care, and you judge the violent and vengeful with the simple words of children. What are human beings compared with your vast, complex creation: the heavenly bodies, the beasts of the earth, the birds of the air and the fish of the sea? By your grace, we are crowned with glory and honor—though you, whose name is majestic, remain our Sovereign Lord!

Opening Prayer

In six days, O God, you created all things, as Wisdom stood by and your Spirit swept over the depths. In six days: light and sky, the seas and dry land, seeds and trees, plants and vegetation, sun and moon, fish and birds, beasts and, last of all, man and woman. And on the seventh day, you rested, thus establishing a rhythm of hallowed rest for the blessing of all things. Therefore, on this day of rest, we seek you and the peace and fruitfulness that proceed from you. Receive, restore, and refresh us, we pray, in your ever-gracious and glorious presence.

Call to Confession

Scripture testifies that, even when the disciples first saw the risen Christ, even as they worshipped him, some doubted. Such doubts are a vestige of the very sin Jesus came to overthrow, but they also reveal that sin and doubt are finally overcome by faith; and as Jesus himself testifies, the Son of Man, when he returns, will be looking for faith on earth. Let us confess our doubts and sins.

Prayer of Confession

Holy God, your goodness is revealed to us in countless ways, but above all in the resurrection of Jesus from the dead; yet we confess we have been slow to believe, selective in our obedience to Christ's authority, and sluggish in fulfilling your commission to baptize and teach the nations. Forgive us for our doubtful, halting ways, and our failure to recognize your constant presence and your authority over all things. Restore to us a clear sense of your purpose for us, that we might render you steadfast, reliable service, for the glory and the pleasure of our triune God.

Declaration of Forgiveness

Friends, believe the good news and rejoice, for by the grace of Christ we are forgiven. Therefore, put things in order; live in agreement with one another; forgive one another and abide in peace; treat one another in a manner befitting the saints of God; and the God of love and peace will be with you.

Presentation of Tithes and Offerings

The whole creation testifies to the vast diversity of the triune God's providence and abundant grace. Yet, the stewardship of creation has been given over to human beings. Who then shall exercise the proper care and dominion, if not those who acknowledge that all authority in heaven and on earth has been given to Jesus Christ? Let us present our offerings in the name of Jesus for the proper administration of his kingdom and toward the fulfillment of his mission on earth.

Prayer of Dedication

Holy, holy, holy God, in Jesus Christ you are with us to the end, and he has charged us to baptize the nations in your triune name, to make disciples, and to teach obedience to your commands. Toward that great end, we tender these humble gifts, knowing they are nothing unless you consecrate them, just as our labors amount to little without you to guide and inspire us, without you to prepare the hearts of those whom we hope to reach and teach, to baptize and bless. Therefore, use these gifts according to your gracious will, that your desired purposes might be accomplished, for your glory.

The Blessing [2 Corinthians 13:13]

The grace of the Lord Jesus Christ,
the love of God,
and the communion of the Holy Spirit
be with all of you.

Proper 4
Ordinary Time 9 / May 29–June 4 (*if after Trinity*)

Genesis 6:9–22; 7:24; 8:14–19
Psalm 46
Romans 1:16–17; 3:22b–28 (29–31)
Matthew 7:21–29

In Preparation for Worship

O God, who makes our wars to cease,
who breaks the bow and shatters the spear,
who speaks to our hearts your words of peace,
who burns our defenses and melts our fear:
You are God! You are holy! You are here!

Call to Worship

Look around you at the state of the world:
God's good creation is corrupted by human sin.
> What shall we do but turn to the Lord?
> For God alone is our hope and our salvation.
Look to the Lord, indeed, O people.
Build your house on the solid rock of Christ.
> If only the world would heed the word of God!
> If only the wise would act upon it!
Look to the works of the Lord and see;

see how God governs the earth and subdues it.
Be still and know that the LORD is God!
> **The LORD of hosts is with us;**
> **the God of Jacob is our refuge!**

Opening Prayer

Eternal God, you are righteous and faithful, just and true. You have proven yourself reliable in times of trouble. Therefore, we seek the shelter of your sure presence, that we might dwell securely with you in your holy presence and praise you for eternity, our everlasting LORD!

Call to Confession

To those who place their faith in Jesus, God gives grace as the gift by which they are justified. There is no distinction among sinners, for all have sinned and fallen short of the glory of God. Let us confess our need of grace, our need of Jesus.

Prayer of Confession

Almighty God, you have set before us your words of truth, yet we have often ignored them or been afraid to trust them. You have shown us your faithfulness and your untiring forbearance, yet we tremble to think how much we have tested them. Cleanse us, O LORD, as you cleansed the world with the flood. Preserve us from the desolation that surrounds us. Give us the faith by which we are justified, the faith of Jesus Christ, that we might forever die to sin and trust in your power to raise us up again, in victory and in joy.

Declaration of Forgiveness

The sacrifice of atonement by the blood of Christ is effective, not by human law or logic, but by love and through faith. God has done this to show that we are saved when our sins are covered over by the blood of Jesus. By passing over the sins we previously committed, God the Father demonstrates perfect divine righteousness, parental compassion, and loving respect for the blood of Jesus the Son, by justifying all whose sins are so covered, all who have the faith of Jesus alive within them, all who place their trust in Christ, for in Christ Jesus we are forgiven. Let no one boast, but let all receive redemption through this unspeakable gift and live forever in reverent thanks to our merciful Lord.

Presentation of Tithes and Offerings

The one who is in right relationship with God will live by faith. Therefore, let us express our faith in God by offering what we have set aside for this purpose, knowing, as we do, that God is our first, our last, and our constant provider.

Prayer of Dedication

O God Most High, you are the author of all peace and the source of a great river of blessings. We are glad that you are our God, and because you are in our midst, we shall not be moved. As nations rise and fall, as troubled hearts melt with fear in tumultuous times, may this act of giving proclaim to the world our confidence in you and tell of your trustworthy and compassionate concern for all in your wonderful creation!

The Blessing

The words of Jesus, the Living Word, are the basis for your whole life: for your thoughts, your utterances, and your actions; so let the righteousness of God go ahead of you, the faith of Christ support you, and the grace of the Holy Spirit bear fruit in you and follow in your wake.

Proper 5
Ordinary Time 10 / June 5–11 (*if after Trinity*)

Genesis 12:1–9
Psalm 33:1–12
Romans 4:13–25
Matthew 9:9–13, 18–26

IN PREPARATION FOR WORSHIP

When we give you glory, O God, we are strengthened in our faith.
When we follow you in faith, you lead us into joy and blessing.
When we call upon your holy name, you swiftly answer and give us peace.
May it be so, Lord. May it ever be so.

CALL TO WORSHIP

The Creator who gives life to the dead
calls us to live a new life.
> **The LORD who creates life from nothing**
> **liberates us for authentic living!**

By the word of the LORD the heavens were made,
and all their hosts by the breath of God.
> **How can we do less than to live in truth,**
> **and to seek to be the people God has called us to be?**

Follow the voice of the God who calls you.
Hope against hope, and come out of your gloom!

> Christ has come that sinners may be saved.
> Rejoice in the Lord. Sing a new song of praise!

Opening Prayer

Blessed One, you are the source of all earthly and eternal life. We come to you, for there is none so gracious as you. You have blessed us and, in your Spirit, we would be a blessing to others. Help us to be good stewards of the faith you have given us and responsive disciples of our Lord Jesus Christ, in whose name we pray.

Call to Confession

The power of sin undercuts all who would place their ultimate hope in themselves, all who presume that their obedience to the law is a sufficient basis for their salvation. For the law itself brings the wrath of God upon the self-righteous; to them faith means nothing, mercy is unnecessary, and the sheer grace of God's loving promises is never received with thanksgiving. Our hope, however, is in holding fast to the Spirit's gracious gift of saving faith in Jesus Christ. In good faith, let us confess our sin.

Prayer of Confession

Merciful God, we acknowledge that we need your healing power and your compassion. We admit that we show few signs of your righteousness, but we manifest many symptoms of persistent spiritual ills: where you desire mercy, we mistake you for a harsh judge; where you have promised us eternal joy, we waver in distrust; where you would bless us with new life, we cling to the old ways of doubt, despair, and death. Heal us, O Lord, of all that harms us. Free us from hurtful habits and thoughtless actions. Restore us by your good grace, and nurture in us the faith of Christ.

Declaration of Forgiveness

Since Christ Jesus has already made the perfect offering for human sin, what sacrifice could we make that would be pleasing to God? Shall we not surrender all doubts? For our God has said, "I desire steadfast love and not sacrifice, the knowledge of God rather than burnt offerings." Therefore, let us love the Lord of life and seek to know God through faith; and let us praise the Lord always, for truly, we are forgiven and justified by the risen Lord Jesus Christ!

Presentation of Tithes and Offerings

God has gone beyond the boundaries to save us, to heal us, to draw us into the kingdom of heaven, where we have a rich heritage, an eternal inheritance with Christ. The earth is full of the steadfast love of the Lord! Therefore, let us enter the streams of God's blessings and share our gifts with the world in the spirit of grace.

Prayer of Dedication

Holy God, you call us away from familiar circumstances to embark on a journey of faith. As we seek you, you bless us with joyful discoveries and hopeful adventures. Help us to risk our settled lives for the sake of exploring new horizons, for telling the world of your good, gracious, and saving work in Jesus. To this end, we dedicate ourselves and these offerings, given in the love of your only Son, our dear Savior and Lord.

The Blessing

God has promised you eternal life, no matter what the doubters have to say. Trust in the promise and follow the voice of the only trustworthy Promisor. Call upon the Spirit who fills you with faith. Hope against hope, and praise the Lord always, for praise befits the upright, and, indeed, you are upright, counted as righteous through sharing in the resurrection of Christ.

Proper 6
Ordinary Time 11 / June 12–18 (*if after Trinity*)

Genesis 18:1–15 (21:1–7)

Psalm 116:1–2, 12–19

Romans 5:1–8

Matthew 9:35—10:8 (9–23)

In Preparation for Worship

Lord of the harvest,
your Son Jesus Christ has instructed us
to ask you to send out laborers to help with your ingathering.
So we come to you in an attitude of humble worship,
to ask that you would indeed send out laborers for this purpose,
and use this hour to equip us with a willing spirit
to complete the work you have given us,
even as you call others to help us reap
in your fruitful fields.

Call to Worship

The kingdom of God is at hand!
Christ is coming to dwell among us and bless us.
> Let the children of God be at peace.
> Let us prepare our hearts and our homes to receive the Lord.
The Son of Man is coming soon

to reward all those who endure in faith.
> **Let us keep faith in God who gave us birth.**
> **Let us worship the LORD who offers us his cup of blessing.**

Opening Prayer

We gather in your presence, O LORD, to declare our love for you. For you hear our prayers, Holy One, and you bless us abundantly! But how shall we fulfill our vows to you who are faithful, even when we are not? May our thankful praise and devoted service be a pleasing sacrifice to you, for you are most worthy, O LORD our God!

Call to Confession

The gracious love of our Savior is such that while we were weak, at the right time, Christ died for the ungodly. This extraordinary love that God shows us has been proven in that while we were still sinners, Christ died for us. The result of Jesus' death is our justification, the forgiveness of all our sins, whether confessed or repressed. For when we repent of sin itself and receive our loving God in faith, the death of Christ is such that sin itself dies with him.

Prayer of Confession

God of compassion, you have commissioned us as your chosen disciples to show mercy to one other and to show forth and proclaim your reign among us. Yet we live more like harassed and helpless sheep, unwilling and unable to follow you. What unworthy words we have spoken, what sinful deeds we have done in your presence! Forgive us in your endless patience and mercy. We confess we cannot fulfill our commission apart from your Spirit. Therefore, renew and re-create us. Reconcile us to one another and to you as you teach us your ways. Fill our hearts anew with the Holy Spirit of our Lord Jesus Christ!

Declaration of Forgiveness

If, in our sin and rebellion, we were once considered enemies of God and were offered peace with God by means of the death of God's Son, how much more, now that we have been made friends with God through this costly reconciliation, will we be saved because of Jesus' marvelous resurrection? If, by Jesus' death, your sins are dissolved, then trust that in his glory, Christ has given and will give you a marvelous new life in the kingdom of heaven. This is the gift of eternal life, and it begins right now!

Presentation of Tithes and Offerings

God is eager and quick to bless all who trust in the divine good will, especially those who have no other reasonable hope of blessing. Even to barren old women like Sarah and tottering old men like Abraham the great God gives laughter, children, new life, and bright hope for the future. To the young, the Holy One gives the promise of a blessed covenant, a sure guidance, and faithful companionship. May nothing ever come between us and our marvelous God! Let us offer up our gifts in demonstration of our ultimate devotion to the blessed and benevolent One, in the name of Jesus Christ.

Prayer of Dedication

Blessed God, we have received much from you, and you have freely given. We cannot begin to repay you for even one of your innumerable gifts, but we can and do try to give as you give: freely, seeking nothing in return. May our only reward be in our hope that our giving gives you joy, that you might see in our humble offerings a reflection of our love for your dear Son, who is your ultimate gift to us and to the world. Bless these gifts to your use and bless us to the service of Jesus Christ's glorious reign over all creation.

The Blessing

You are authorized agents of the kingdom of God,
because you bear the name of Christ.
You have authority to tell the news of Christ Jesus,

because you are endowed with the Holy Spirit.
As the love of God has been poured into your hearts,
go and do works of love, speaking God's words of love
in the spirit of peace.

Proper 7
Ordinary Time 12 / June 19–25 (*if after Trinity*)

Genesis 21:8–21
Psalm 86:1–10, 16–17
Romans 6:1b–11
Matthew 10:24–39

In Preparation for Worship

To you, O Lord, I lift up my soul.
You make my heart exceedingly glad!
For you, my God, are good and forgiving,
loving and kind to all who call on you.
There is no one like you, O merciful God!

Call to Worship

Nothing is covered that will not be uncovered.
Nothing is secret that will not become known.
> The one who acknowledges Christ, Christ will acknowledge.
> The one who denies him will be denied.
What the Lord speaks to you in the dark, tell in the light.
What the Spirit whispers to you, proclaim from the housetops!
> **We know that Christ, being raised from the dead,**
> **will never die again. Death no longer has dominion over him!**
The death he died, he died to sin.

But the life he lives, he lives to God!
> **Therefore, we too shall consider ourselves dead to sin and alive to God in Christ Jesus our Lord!**

Opening Prayer

God of compassion, Author of creation, apart from whom no sparrow can fall: Nothing escapes your notice, your pity, or your tender love. Make us ever conscious of your perfect love for us, that we might have courage to face every challenge and to faithfully bear the cross. May we always, even in the face of death, trust in your great mercy for the gift of eternal life in Christ.

Call to Confession

How can we who have died to sin go on living in it? Do you not know that all of us who have been baptized into Christ Jesus have been baptized into his death? Therefore, let us consign all of our sins to Christ, who died in order that sin itself should die.

Prayer of Confession [see Psalm 86]

Incline your ear, O Lord, and answer your people, for in your holy presence we realize just how poor and needy we are. We confess we have too often put ourselves forward, not for service, but in selfishness; afraid of losing our lives for your sake, we have expended untold time, energy, and resources on self-preservation; fearing loss, we have clutched things that are better relinquished; failing to trust you for the gift of life, we have shrunk from your sacrificial calling. Forgive us and be gracious to us, O Lord. Give us courage and faith to follow you with renewed joy, loyalty, and devotion. For you are good and forgiving, O Lord, abounding in steadfast love to all who call on you.

Declaration of Forgiveness

Do not be afraid; for your merciful God has heard your prayers. God, who gives us eyes to see, also displays the plenteous provisions with which our needs are met in Jesus Christ. For all of us who have been baptized into Christ Jesus were baptized into his death, buried with him by baptism into death, and raised with him from death by the glory of God the Father, that we too might walk in newness of life. Therefore, consider yourselves dead to sin and alive to God in Christ Jesus! Thanks be to God!

Presentation of Tithes and Offerings

If our heavenly Father has every hair accounted for and his eye on every sparrow, what shortage shall we fear? If the disciple is not above the teacher, what sacrifice can anyone offer to match or exceed the sacrifice of Christ? None! Nevertheless, let us follow our Lord and teacher by laying down our lives for one another, that we might be like the teacher; let us, in all our ways, acknowledge Christ, and discover in our giving that Christ is indeed with us and leading us along the way to eternal life.

Prayer of Dedication

Surely, there is none like you among the gods, O Lord, nor are there any works like yours. For you have heard our cries of supplication. You have shown us great favor; indeed, you have helped and comforted your people. Therefore, in imitation of your generous ways, we offer these gifts to you, that the world might see how graciously you deal with those whom you regard, through Christ, as your own beloved children.

The Blessing

Have no fear! But trust in the God who has raised Jesus from the dead. Take up your cross. Follow the one over whom death has no dominion. Live as those who have already lost—and gained—everything,
as those who have found the new life in Christ!

Proper 8
Ordinary Time 13 / June 26–July 2

Genesis 22:1–14
Psalm 13
Romans 6:12–23
Matthew 10:40–42

In Preparation for Worship

When I gather with these others, I see you in all,
for yours is the Image in which all are made.
When I gather with these others, I am joined to you,
for this is the Body you form anew this day.
When I gather with these others, I welcome you,
and I welcome the One who sent you.

Call to Worship

The Lord provides for those who keep faith.
Trust in God's mercy, for the costliest gift is given you.
> **God has dealt bountifully with us.**
> **The Son of God has been offered up for us.**

Rejoice in your eternal salvation.
Sing to the Lord with your whole heart!
> **The Lord gives light to our darkened eyes.**
> **God's free gift of grace is eternal life in Christ.**

Lift your hearts in obedience to God.
Present yourselves humbly and receive your sanctification.
> Great indeed are the rewards of faith.
> Our joy is to know, to love, and to serve the living LORD.

OPENING PRAYER

Bountiful God, you notice every act of charity and kindness, and you are just in remembering and rewarding those who do them. Help us to commit ourselves in thought, word, and deed to remaining free from slavery to sin, and to serving you as your trusted children, freely bound together in love and truth, joyfully destined for eternal life in and with Jesus Christ, in whose name we pray.

CALL TO CONFESSION

Do not let sin dominate your lives, for the wages of sin is death! But those who would choose eternal life must turn from serving self to serving God. As we confess our sin, may the One who brought Jesus from death to new life remove your sin and bless you with mercy and grace.

PRAYER OF CONFESSION

Living God, our mistakes tell the story of how the sin in our lives only leads to greater and greater strife and iniquity. Nothing we have done in impurity has ever worked to our advantage; nothing of which we are ashamed can ever testify on our behalf. Help us put all wickedness to death, that we might offer our bodies as instruments of righteousness. Forgive us for all our past failings; set us free to live under your grace; fill us with the Spirit of Christ; and set us on the true path to eternal life.

DECLARATION OF FORGIVENESS

Thanks be to God that we, having once been slaves of sin, have been released from its grip; we are free to become slaves of righteousness, free to become fully obedient from the heart to God's government of grace, free to enjoy the gift of eternal life in Christ Jesus our Lord! From now on present your bodies to the Lord as instruments of righteousness and prepare to reap the good fruit of your sanctification.

Presentation of Tithes and Offerings

Nothing we give away goes unnoticed by God. No gift, small or large, is overlooked or forgotten. No kind word, no gesture of love, no act of sharing will go unrewarded. Nevertheless, do not let thoughts of reward be your motivation for giving, but the prospect of doing a kindness for our living, loving Lord, who is ever among us and perceiving us through the eyes of our neighbors, friends, and strangers.

Prayer of Dedication

How can we ever show you the depth of faith you deserve, O God? Surely there is nothing of this world with which we cannot trust you, for you have created every material thing we enjoy and fulfilled our every spiritual need in offering up your Son Jesus Christ for our salvation. You are the supreme Giver. Therefore, we surrender these gifts to you, that you might bless them and direct us in their use. May this ministry in your holy name be a sure sign of your gracious presence in the world, and your gracious, self-giving love on behalf of the world. We ask this is Jesus' name.

The Blessing

Go forth prepared to see the Lord in the children,
to meet the Lord in the upright,
to welcome the Lord in the godly,
and to delight as the Lord appears in the most unlikely places.
May the Holy Spirit give you the grace and the peace to go in love
and serve the Lord Jesus,
wherever you go, in whomever you meet.

Proper 9
Ordinary Time 14 / July 3–9

Genesis 24:34–38, 42–49, 58–67
Psalm 45:10–17 OR Song of Solomon 2:8–13
Romans 7:15–25a
Matthew 11:16–19, 25–30

In Preparation for Worship

Lord Jesus, you have invited us to set aside our burdens,
to come to you, to learn from you, to rest in you.
You have offered us your light yoke,
your gentle nature, your humble heart.
Thus do we come to you, O Lord,
praying that you will relieve our minds,
unburden our hearts,
and lighten our steps
as we come.

Call to Worship

Hear, O bride of Christ, consider and incline your ear.
For Christ your King desires your beauty.
> **Since he is our Lord, let us bow to him.**
> **With joy and gladness, let us enter the palace of the King.**
In the place of ancestors you, O Lord, shall have many heirs;

you will make them reign in all the earth.
> **May your name be celebrated in all generations.**
> **May the peoples praise you forever and ever!**

OR

The voice of the beloved speaks and says to me,
"Arise, my love, my fair one, and come away."
> **Look, there he stands, behind our wall,**
> **gazing in through the lattice.**

The vines are in blossom;
the flowers appear on the earth.
> **The voice of the turtledove is heard in the land;**
> **the time for singing has come.**

Opening Prayer

O Lord God of Abraham, you know our every word before we have spoken, and you faithfully act upon our prayers when they are offered in trust, according to the wise counsel of your Holy Spirit. Acquaint us anew with your lightness and the grace of your service, that we may be unburdened by the weight of the world and its cares, and find ourselves joyfully in the presence of your Son Jesus Christ, where we may learn his gentle, humble, restful, and refreshing ways.

Call to Confession

How often do our actions contradict God's will! Surely the mind and the flesh are at odds with one another. For even when we want to do what is good, evil lies close at hand. If at times we do not even understand our own conduct but do the very thing we know to be wrong, we also know that the contradiction does not accord with our true nature as children of God, but arises from the sin that remains within us. Therefore, let us confess our sin to God, who alone can give us rest.

Prayer of Confession

O God, our heavenly Father, you are holy and righteous, revealing your Son to children, to the humble and the faithful. Yet, we confess, we are blinded by pride, worldly wisdom, and the presumption that we are in complete control; we see the same faults in others that we harbor in ourselves. Surely, nothing good resides in our flesh, for we find that when we desire to do what is right, we cannot do it, for sin soon gains the upper hand, and we fail to avail ourselves of your sovereign power and will. Forgive us, O God, and remove the yoke of sin from our shoulders. Place upon us your light yoke of peace, grace, and joy in Christ, knowing that you favor the lowly and give victory to those who confess their need of your Son, in whose name we pray.

Declaration of Forgiveness

Hear and rejoice in this good news: For though we all have sinned, labored, and languished in such a wretched state, we have a redeemer, Jesus Christ, who has rescued us from this body of death. Let us live no longer as slaves to sin, but as those who are chosen, beloved, and desired by God. Thanks be to God through Jesus Christ our Lord!

Presentation of Tithes and Offerings

All things have been handed over to Jesus Christ by our heavenly Father, though Christ and his kingdom remain hidden to the world until God chooses to reveal them. We, however, not only acknowledge Christ as Lord; we participate in his kingdom when we offer our gifts in his name and devote them to his ministry and for the glory of our triune God.

Prayer of Dedication

We thank you, O God our Father, Lord of heaven and earth, for though you have hidden the ways of your kingdom from the wise and the crafty in this world, you have revealed them to your children, according to your gracious will. As you faithfully led our ancestors in the ancient and everlasting way and greatly blessed them, may your blessing be upon these gifts as you direct us in their use. Grant us success in your service, as you

alone know how to supply and measure it, that your will might be done,
in Jesus' name.

The Blessing

May you, who are chosen and beloved of God,
increase and become thousands.
May your children and heirs become myriads of faithful saints who,
in the name of Jesus Christ, gain victory over all worldly snares
and, in the power of the Holy Spirit,
find strength to endure until the King of heaven comes.

Proper 10
Ordinary Time 15 / July 10–16

Genesis 25:19–34

Psalm 119:105–12

Romans 8:1–11

Matthew 13:1–9, 18–23

In Preparation for Worship

O God our very Life, source of every blessing,
our compassionate companion, our eternal destination:
we come as we are to render you due praise,
trusting in you to renew and refresh us.
Humble and broken through we are,
we lift up your holy name.

Call to Worship

Come to God, who has raised Jesus from the dead.
This same God gives life to your mortal bodies.
> **Our Creator lives among us.**
> **The Holy Spirit dwells within us.**

The Word of God is your promised heritage.
The light of Christ will show you the path to joy.
> **The Spirit of God is the source of our life.**
> **Let us incline our hearts to our eternal God.**

Set your minds on the things of the Spirit.
For to do so is to have life and peace.
> **Accept our offering of praise, O Lord.**
> **Give us life according to your Word!**

Opening Prayer

O Lord our God, we desire to be your good, rich soil, open and receptive to the good news of Christ Jesus, that your Word may take root and thrive in our midst, that your kingdom of promise may be fruitful and produce a harvest of obedience, and that the world might see in us the joyful and glorious benefits of knowing you, our living, loving Lord.

Call to Confession

Though we may be severely afflicted, the Spirit gives life to those who do not forget or neglect God's gracious Word. Let nothing divert your attention from God, and let no sin dissuade you from seeking his presence, but have faith and surrender to the Holy Spirit's goodness at work in all circumstances. With such faith, let us confess our sin.

Prayer of Confession

Redeeming God, we confess that we frequently set our minds on matters of the flesh and fail to submit ourselves to the rule of your life-giving Spirit. How can we please you when we shrink from trouble and persecution, when we lack the courage and faith to withstand times of testing? How can we please you when we allow the cares of the world to lure us away from you, when we so easily surrender your blessing and joy? Forgive us, O God, and give us courage, strength, and healing! Help us redirect our aims and our attitudes toward you. Let the seal of your Holy Spirit remain upon us and the Spirit of Christ abide within us, that we might share in the eternal life of the One who died to set us free from sin.

Declaration of Forgiveness

According to the Spirit of Christ, you are now free from the law of sin and death, since there is now no longer any condemnation for those who are in Christ Jesus. If you are in Christ and Christ is in you, though the body is dead because of sin, nevertheless, the Spirit is your new life because of the righteousness won for us by Jesus. The One who has died for you and forgiven you now dwells within you and will surely give you the gift of eternal life! Take heart, be at peace, and know that you are truly free.

Presentation of Tithes and Offerings

We have an everlasting heritage in God's eternal Word. We have a spirit of joy that is ours when we set our minds on the things of the Spirit. We have a covenant with God that is fulfilled in the Lord Jesus Christ. What do our worldly goods amount to in light of this blessedness? Shall we not then share them cheerfully for the sake of spreading this good news to the world?

Prayer of Dedication

God of the Covenant, you withhold no good thing from those who trust you. You give every spiritual blessing to those who set their minds on your Spirit. Receive these humble gifts and sanctify them by your gracious hand, that they might be used to your holy purpose, by your beloved people, for the glory of Jesus Christ our Savior, in whose mighty name we pray.

The Blessing

Go in the peace that only the love of God can give you;
take the Word of God deep into your hearts;
consider it in the eternal light of Jesus;
nurture it with prayer in the Spirit of new life;
and by your love for God and neighbor,
show forth the glory of the risen Christ.

Proper 11
Ordinary Time 16 / July 17–23

Genesis 28:10–19a
Psalm 139:1–12, 23–24
Romans 8:12–25
Matthew 13:24–30, 36–43

In Preparation for Worship

We long to be our true selves, O God,
as you have created us and desire us to be.
Yet, for the time being, evil lies close at hand,
as we await the day when all sin and wickedness
will be uprooted and burned.
Keep us, O Lord, until that day,
that we may shine like the sun
in your glorious kingdom!

Call to Worship

Come to God, the giver of life,
for the Lord knows you better than you know yourself.
> **We come to the One who knows us completely.**
> **May God lead us in the everlasting way.**
The Lord's hand is upon you,
to guide and teach you, and to hold you fast!

> We come to the One who is in all and through all.
> May the love of Christ Jesus shine brightly within us.

Hope in the Lord, O children of God,
for the Holy Spirit testifies that we are joint heirs with Christ.
> We hope in the Holy One, the giver of freedom,
> whose glory will redeem all of our sufferings.

Opening Prayer

O God of our Ancestors, you are forever faithful. You are always with us, and you keep us close to you wherever we go. You will neither leave us nor forsake us, though we have been only dimly aware of your constancy. May our conduct be ever pleasing to your watchful eyes; may our words be in concert with your Holy Word; and may our hearts ever sing for joy at your wondrous, unfailing love, revealed to us so perfectly in Christ Jesus!

Call to Confession

Is not the Lord with us in ways we cannot see? Has not the Lord blessed us in ways we do not comprehend? Our knowledge and perception of God is as quickly clouded by sin as it is sharpened by trustful confession of our errors and of God's gracious goodness. Let us therefore confess together.

Prayer of Confession

O God, we admit we are an impatient people, ever straining ahead in pursuit of fleeting rewards. Yet, at the first sign of adversity, we fall back into fear. Where our eager longing for your glory should govern us, we have allowed our sins to enslave us and our doubts to entrap us. Forgive us, O God. May your Holy Spirit search our hearts, dispel every evil thought, and awaken in us the hopeful expectation of new life in your new creation.

Declaration of Forgiveness

We are debtors, not to the flesh, but to Jesus Christ and to the Spirit of God who leads us and who testifies with us that we are children of God, heirs of God and joint heirs with Christ, that we may also be glorified with Christ. And the glory about to be revealed is one for which we wait with patient yet eager longing, knowing that we already have the first fruits of the Spirit, and we shall undoubtedly obtain the freedom of the glory of the children of God. Therefore, be at peace in the assurance of your free and glorious future, and give thanks to God.

Presentation of Tithes and Offerings

Since we have the spirit of adoption, as children and heirs of God, we have no fear of sharing, but we have the promise of blessing. Therefore, let us sow good seed in the harvest field of God, knowing that the Lord himself will give the growth and ensure a good harvest, in which we ourselves, the children of the kingdom, are his produce.

Prayer of Dedication

Our heavenly Father, there is such resistance to your Word in the world, but we trust in your Son and your coming kingdom to bring home the glorious harvest of the righteous. Thus, we offer these gifts as our witness and our sure hope that, whatever adversity arises, your good seed will indeed bear good fruit, and your chosen will be glorified like the sun at the end of the age. May our gifts and our labors be joined to your redeeming work, for it is in the name of Jesus Christ that we would seek and serve for the sake of your glory.

The Blessing

The Lord is with you and will keep you wherever you go;
Jesus Christ will not leave you, but will fulfill what God has promised you.
Therefore, know that the blessings of heaven attend you,
and may the Holy Spirit increase you and lead you in the way everlasting.

Proper 12
Ordinary Time 17 / July 24–30

Genesis 29:15–28

Psalm 105:1–11, 45b OR Psalm 128

Romans 8:26–39

Matthew 13:31–33, 44–52

IN PREPARATION FOR WORSHIP

Loving God, forgiving Christ, enlivening Spirit:
fill me, bear with me, direct my prayers,
and bring your new creation to completion!

CALL TO WORSHIP

Come, you who seek the LORD.
Let your hearts rejoice! Glory in God's holy name.
> **Sing to God; sing praises to the LORD.**
> **Tell the world of God's wonderful works.**

Come, seek the presence of God continually.
Let your souls draw strength from the LORD.
> **Trust in God; keep faith in the LORD.**
> **God is at work in all things for your good.**

Come, all who fear the LORD.
Happy are those who walk in the ways of God.
> **Love the LORD! Let us overcome all things through the cross.**
> **For nothing can separate us from God's love in Christ Jesus.**

OR

We do not know how to pray as we ought.
> **Holy Spirit, help us in our weakness.**

We do know that all things work together for good for those who love God.
> **Creator God, search our hearts.**

We are known and elected to be conformed to Christ's image.
> **Jesus Christ, pray for us,**
> **that nothing may separate us from your love.**

Opening Prayer

In faith, we see how you work on us, O God. In hope, we consider how you pray for us. In truth, we know that you govern us, O Lord. In love, we trust that you have saved us for the eventual completion of the joy of Jesus Christ. Thus, we gather to seek your presence, to rejoice in your wondrous works, and to glorify your holy name.

Call to Confession

The Lord is our God; his judgments are in all the earth. He is mindful of his covenant forever. According to his covenant and purpose, he has predestined those whom he foreknew to be conformed to the image of his Son, Jesus Christ, who has suffered to set us free from sin. And those for whom he has provided, those whom he predestined in this way, he has also called and justified and glorified. Happy is everyone who fears the Lord. Let us, in gratitude and confidence, penitence and faith, confess our sins to our provident God.

Prayer of Confession

God of grace and glory, you have called us to be conformed to the image of Jesus Christ, yet we have often failed to live and behave in a Christ-like manner. We are quick to forget the teachings of Jesus and we are reluctant to trust them to work for our good. Forgive us, O God, for our disloyalty and lack of faith. Justify us by your grace. Bless us according to your will, that we might flourish and give you glory.

OR

Living God, you have revealed to us things hidden from the beginning of the world. Yet our eyes cannot see you, our ears cannot hear you, our senses have grown dull with sin, our bodies weary with ceaseless strivings. Save us, O God, from foolish diversions and wasteful pursuits. Correct us, O Christ, and conform us to your image. Help us, O Spirit, for we are weak and we know not how to pray.

Declaration of Forgiveness

Truly, the Holy Spirit helps us in our weakness, interceding for us with sighs too deep for words. Thus, even as we pray, the very Spirit of God prays for us as well, according to God's sovereign will. Therefore, if God is for us, who is against us? He who did not withhold his own Son, but gave him up for all of us, will he not, with Christ, also give us everything else? Who will bring any charge against God's elect? It is God who justifies. Therefore, in all things we are surely more than conquerors through him who loved us, and nothing will be able to separate us from the love of God in Christ Jesus our Lord.

Presentation of Tithes and Offerings

Like a mustard seed that grows into the greatest of shrubs; like a little yeast that leavens a whole batch of dough; like treasure hidden in a field; like a merchant who sells all in order to purchase one pearl of great value, God does great things in the kingdom of heaven, often with just the slightest provisions; meanwhile, those who have been trained for the kingdom are like the master of a household who brings out of his treasure both new and old things. Let us present our treasures to God, whether they be small or large, that the King of heaven might perform mighty works with them and be glorified.

Prayer of Dedication

We give thanks to you, O Lord; we call on your name. For though we do not always know what to pray for, and we can only sow our seeds in weakness, nevertheless, we have your Spirit sighing deeply, searching hearts, revealing your will, and ensuring that all things work together for good for those who love you, those whom you have called. May our use of these gifts likewise cooperate with your good purposes, that your deeds and your wonderful works might be made known among all peoples, and that all the world might learn to sing your praises.

THE BLESSING [Psalm 128:5–6; see also Galatians 6:16]

The LORD bless you from Zion.
May you see the prosperity of Jerusalem
all the days of your life.
May you see your children's children.
Peace be upon the Israel of God!

Proper 13
Ordinary Time 18 / July 31–August 6

Genesis 32:22–31
Psalm 17:1–7, 15
Romans 9:1–5
Matthew 14:13–21

In Preparation for Worship

Holy One, we seek the bread of your presence;
we have come to lean on you for strength;
we trust in your victorious grace.
Therefore, let the world see and recognize,
for your glory, that our hope is not misplaced.

Call to Worship

Call upon the Lord, O people.
Let your voice be heard in heaven!
> Show us your steadfast love, O Lord.
> For we seek refuge in you.

Call upon the Lord. Place your trust in God.
Ask the Lord for an eternal blessing.
> Show us your face, O wondrous God.
> Let your will for us become our greatest joy.

Call upon the Lord, O people.

Trust in God who anticipates all your needs.
> **Grant us true bread for our journey.**
> **Fill us with your Word, that our hunger may be satisfied.**

Opening Prayer

Blessed God, we gather in the name of Jesus the Christ, mindful that you have done great things for us in your Son. Our memories cannot fully recall, our minds cannot comprehend how many and great are the blessings you have spoken over us. We simply know that you are an immeasurably gracious God: kind, generous, faithful, and loving. Therefore, we worship you, for you alone are good and true and worthy of praise.

Call to Confession

Who is free of deceitful motivations? Who is perfectly pure of heart? Can anyone claim to be truly in the right? Does not our vindication come from Christ alone? Surely, though we live in the presence of our holy God, we are spared condemnation in order to learn a godly way of living, to be blessed with a righteousness that does not come from ourselves, but from God. Therefore, let us confess our sins to God and look to heaven for the abundant grace on which we so depend.

Prayer of Confession

Faithful God, we confess that we do not easily submit to you, but we have preferred to govern ourselves. We have resisted your will and sought ways to avoid bringing ourselves under your authority. We are often afraid of letting go of familiar ways, even though they are deficient and cannot bear fruit for your kingdom. Forgive us for our willful disobedience, our rigid resistance, our shallow faith, our lack of trust. Help us open ourselves to you, that we might learn to exchange the empty promises of this world for the sure promise of salvation and eternal life in Christ.

Declaration of Forgiveness

Christ Jesus is a compassionate Savior, who came to heal the sick, to feed the hungry, to free the oppressed, and to impart God's righteousness to humble human beings. The grace of God is such that you are never beyond the reach of Christ. Blessed are those who trust in God's patient love. And blessed is God forever, whose nature it is to forgive us, heal us, and refresh us through the communion of the Holy Spirit and with the Bread of Life and Truth.

Presentation of Tithes and Offerings

If we knew all the spiritual blessings that await us in the kingdom of heaven as God's adopted children, we would find precious few material things, if any, worth holding on to. As an act of faith in God and in the staggering abundance of the kingdom of heaven, let us offer our gifts, that we might actively participate in God's ministry to this hungry world.

Prayer of Dedication

God of Compassion, you are quick to anticipate our needs and to provide for us plentifully. With confidence in your grace, we offer you this portion of our provisions, that we might give, in our small way, as you give in such large and wonderful ways. Sanctify these gifts and guide us in their use for your ministry of kindness and compassion.

The Blessing

Go with the guidance of the Spirit in your conscience;
speak the truth in the love of Christ;
and may the gifts of God be at your disposal,
all for the sake of the kingdom of God!

Proper 14
Ordinary Time 19 / August 7–13

Genesis 37:1–4, 12–28

Psalm 105:1–6, 16–22, 45b

Romans 10:5–15

Matthew 14:22–33

In Preparation for Worship

Our Lord Jesus Christ, we call upon you for our salvation,
for you are generous to all, and you are never far away.
May the words of our lips and the faith of our hearts
ever be true to you, O Lord of all!

Call to Worship

Seek the Lord and rejoice!
Tell the world of God's wonderful works!
> **Jesus is risen! We declare it is true and trust it in our hearts.**
> **All who call on his name shall be saved!**

Give thanks to the Lord. Sing God's praises.
How beautiful are the feet of the one who brings good news!
> **Jesus is Lord! We confess it to the world!**
> **But how will they believe it, unless we proclaim it?**

The Word of God is very near you!
Christ is on your lips and in your hearts!

Jesus is the righteous One we proclaim.
By this Word of faith we are saved.

Opening Prayer

Holy One, you are Lord of sea and sky. You call us to walk by faith, you lead us into the unknown, yet you are always with us, and you will not fail us. We live among many who do not know you or know to trust you. Therefore, we worship you, that we might witness to you, draw strength from you, take solace in you, and find courage and hope for this life of faith.

Call to Confession

Hear these bold promises from Holy Scripture: No one who trusts in Jesus Christ as Lord will ever be put to shame. But if you confess with your lips that Jesus is Lord and trust in your heart that God raised him from the dead, you will be saved. Therefore, by all means, let us believe it and confess it!

Prayer of Confession

Saving God, we confess that our eyes are heavy, our hearts are faint, our minds often entertain fearful thoughts, and our eyes often look away from Jesus, though he is indeed the Lord of life. We admit that our faith is timid and easily troubled, that we frequently open the door to doubts, and that we soon lose sight of your constant, encouraging presence. Forgive us, O God. Help us step forth boldly, with our eyes fixed upon your risen Son, our feet firmly grounded on your revealed truth, our hearts enlightened by your Spirit with the assurance of your love, your gracious humility, and the certain promise of eternal life with you, our triune God.

Declaration of Forgiveness

God is ever ahead of us, making provision for us before we even know what our needs will be. So it is with our need for forgiveness and salvation.

The Word has not been placed at such a distance that we must despair or wonder how to attain it, but the person of Jesus Christ is that saving Word. Christ is the very road we walk, and all the while he has both gone before us and accompanied us along the way; Christ has suffered on our behalf and as an example for us to follow; Christ has provided for our future, and yet he remains present at our side, on our lips, and in our hearts. Know that the promises of God are trustworthy and true. Claim your salvation in Christ and be at peace.

Presentation of Tithes and Offerings

The Lord is generous to all who call out in faith. Christ is near to the trustful at heart. The benefits of God cannot be bought, or kept, or hidden, or hoarded, but those who step out and walk in faith will soon reap the rewards of faith. Let us offer our gifts in faith.

Prayer of Dedication

Our Holy Maker, your righteousness so abounds in your creation that your light ever shines before our eyes; your Word so resounds throughout your creation that your wisdom ever rings in our ears. As we release our hold on these small things and surrender them to you, so wash over us with your grace and mercy that we might forget all we have done, rejoice in what you have done, and remind the world of your goodness in Christ Jesus!

The Blessing

The Word of God attends you.
Therefore, attend to the Word of God always.
Go forth in peace to proclaim the good news,
that others might hear, believe in, and follow Jesus Christ,
the sovereign Son of God.

Proper 15
Ordinary Time 20 / August 14–20

Genesis 45:1–15

Psalm 133

Romans 11:1–2a, 29–32

Matthew 15:(10–20) 21–28

In Preparation for Worship

Giver of Eternal Life, as you call us to be one body
serving in a royal priesthood,
anoint us with your Holy Spirit,
that the glory, honor, and praise we offer you
may be undiminished by human sin,
and that your name may be exalted
by our united voice upraised.

Call to Worship

We come from prisons of disobedience,
> to glorify God, our protector and provider.

We come in search of the One who gives real food,
> though there be famine in the land.

We come from many nations,
> for there is but One who can purify our hearts:

the same One who calls us here to worship.
> Amen. We come, Lord Jesus, Holy Word of God!

Opening Prayer

Holy God, who saves us to be a holy remnant: claim our hearts for burning in the cleansing fire of your Spirit, that the testimony of our lives might be pure, truthful words, and the fruits we produce might be holy, righteous works, a harvest of grace, mercy, and forgiveness, in the name of our Redeemer and gracious Lord Jesus.

Call to Confession

We bring our faults and failures to the LORD, trusting that when we confess them before him, we are set free from guilt, given a clear conscience, and blessedly unburdened. Come, let us confess our sin, with our hopes fixed on the good nature of our gracious God.

Prayer of Confession

O God, who knows all that we have ever said or done, we confess that we have erected facades in order to garner the world's empty praise. O Christ, who endures every harsh word we speak against our enemies, friends, family, and neighbors, we have tried to deny our guilt and to deflect the blame for our sins. O Holy Spirit, who judges every thought and intention of the heart, we have slandered, cursed, and complained; we have failed to love as you would have us love. Holy, triune God, purge our lives of disloyalty and hypocrisy, shame and deceit, guilt and persistent despair. Set us free from the power of sin, and renew us by your abundant grace, in Jesus' name.

Declaration of Forgiveness

The forgiveness of God is the story of loyalty returning, the drama of idolaters converting, the justice of evil hearts breaking, the wild dance of prisoners escaping. In the name of our Lord and Savior Jesus Christ, I tell you: we are forgiven. Therefore, do not return to the former ways, but take up the new life in Christ!

Presentation of Tithes and Offerings

With purity of heart and unity of spirit, let us return to God a remnant of the abundance with which we have been blessed, and let us ask the Lord to consecrate these gifts for the outworking of God's wonderful plan for a new creation in Jesus Christ.

Prayer of Dedication

You, O God, are the source, the wellspring of all goodness, our only hope of freedom and salvation. We offer you these gifts, along with our service, energy, and grateful love. May the world come to acknowledge you through our use of these gifts. May your purpose be fulfilled in our common, yet holy, life in Christ.

The Blessing

How very good and pleasant it is
when kindred live together in unity!
Be united, therefore, in the one sacred purpose
to which you have been called,
and begin today the living of a blessed,
holy, and eternal life in Christ.

Proper 16
Ordinary Time 21 / August 21–27

Exodus 1:8—2:10

Psalm 124

Romans 12:1–8

Matthew 16:13–20

IN PREPARATION FOR WORSHIP

Almighty God, you have built your church upon
the inspired testimony of your disciples.
Come, teach and inspire us,
that we might likewise testify,
with reverent worship and spirited speech,
in praise of our Lord Jesus Christ, the Son of the living God,
and that our words and deeds on earth might yield
heavenly riches for your eternal realm.

CALL TO WORSHIP

Come and seek the God who saves,
    for the LORD has proven faithful and true!
God rescued the child Moses from
Pharaoh's condemnation of Israel's innocents,
    so the infant Moses nursed at his own mother's breast.
God fought for David against a rising tide of enemies.

"Our help is in the name of the LORD,
> who made heaven and earth."

God revealed Jesus as the Messiah, the Son of the living God,
> who entrusted the keys of heaven to his church.

Come and seek the God who saves,
> for the LORD has proven faithful and true!

Opening Prayer

God of the exodus, by whose grace alone we escape the slavery of sin and the penalty of death, help us view the remainder of our lives as a living sacrifice, fruitful and flourishing, that your name might be exalted as the God who blesses the obedient and forgives the penitent, for the sake of your Son, Jesus the Christ.

Call to Confession

This is your spiritual worship: to present your bodies as a living sacrifice, holy and acceptable to God. Therefore, cast off your conformity to the world. Let us confess our sins and open our minds to the transformation with which we are blessed, even as we place our trust in God to forgive us.

Prayer of Confession

Living God, we confess that we have bound ourselves by vain speech and careless words, empowering forces that would cause us to shudder if we knew whereof we spoke. Forgive our thoughtless misuse of language; convert our speech from duplicity to truthful testimony, from idle talk to inspired proclamation, that our lives may not be wasted in servitude, but liberated for service to your good, acceptable, and perfect will, and for the glory of the name above all names: Jesus.

Declaration of Forgiveness

It was once thought the Messiah would come bringing political freedom, in the here and now, to the oppressed people of a tiny nation. But Jesus Christ works a much larger transformation, one that has eternal implications. Christ came to set us free, to loose earthly as well as heavenly bonds, and he promised that the gates of hell would not prevail against this liberating proclamation of the church. The Lord has not given his people as prey to the enemy, but has forgiven us in Christ; thus, we are transformed by the good news of this glorious freedom. Claim the gospel for yourselves and proclaim it to the world! In Jesus Christ, we are forgiven! Thanks be to God!

Presentation of Tithes and Offerings

The gifts we have from God come from across the spiritual and vocational spectrum: some are cheerful, some compassionate, some diligent, some faithful; some are teachers, some leaders, some prophets, ministers, and preachers; some are gracious, some are generous; all according to the particular and abundant blessings that we have received from God. Let us offer to God and share with one another what we have received.

Prayer of Dedication

Take these gifts, O Blessed One, for they were blessings when you gave them to us. May they be blessed again as we return them to you, in hopes that their use will honor your name, encourage the proclamation of Christ, and advance the redeeming work of your Spirit in this broken world.

The Blessing

May God inspire you with the compassion of Christ.
May Christ equip you for the work of the Spirit.
May the Spirit fill you with the love of God
and the joy of telling others the liberating good news—
that Jesus is our promised Savior and Lord of the new creation.

Proper 17
Ordinary Time 22 / August 28–September 3

Exodus 3:1–15
Psalm 105:1–6, 23–26, 45c
Romans 12:9–21
Matthew 16:21–28

IN PREPARATION FOR WORSHIP

O Holy One, in whose name is life itself,
as we approach your presence,
remind us of heavenly things,
that we might be free from worldly concerns,
free to take up the cross with Jesus and follow him
to your coming kingdom.

CALL TO WORSHIP

Holy LORD, you heard Israel cry under the yoke of slavery.
> **Hear our cry, O great I AM.**

Jesus Christ, you ransomed many with your death.
> **Risen Son of God, come again in glory.**

Holy Spirit, you overcome evil with good.
> **Unite your church in the bonds of peace.**

God of our ancestors, you have suffered with us
from generation to generation.

Proper 17—Ordinary Time 22

May your loving presence among us
bring honor and glory to your holy name.

Opening Prayer

Holy God, we know that fire burns, yet the bush that burned with your presence as you spoke to Moses was not consumed. So preserve us, O Lord, though we are parched and dry; saturate and refresh us with your presence. By your grace, and by the life that is in your name, let us not be consumed, but filled with your Spirit and newly inspired to fulfill your purpose for us.

Call to Confession

Holiness and unholiness do not naturally mix, for God's divine nature and our human nature are as different as can be. Yet in Jesus Christ, we know that God's nature and perfected human nature were fully alive, fully present, fully at home together; moreover, Jesus—though sinless—was not aloof from sinners. Therefore, we have hope that though we sin and our sin is not acceptable to God, yet we ourselves are accepted, since Christ sees fit to love us despite our sin. In the good hope of forgiveness, let us confess our sin to God.

Prayer of Confession

Liberating God, we know the wage we earn for sin, any sin, is death, and we confess that we have sinned against your sacred name. Yet, in Christ you are our sure deliverer. From slavery to sin and from slavery to self, you release us. Forgive us, O Lord. Enlist our fresh loyalty and obedience to your commands, that we might remain free of former habits of transgression and past patterns of regression, and boldly surrender our lives in order to find new life in Jesus Christ, in whose name we pray.

Declaration of Forgiveness

God sees our miseries. God hears our cries. God knows our sufferings. Just as God delivered Israel from cruel Egyptian taskmasters and brought them to the broad land of promise, Christ has come with a clear purpose: to deliver us from habitual, hereditary sin into authentic being, from the slavery of despair to joyful, fruitful, life-giving hope. Forgiveness is yours, if you will but have it; you are free to begin a new life in Christ!

Presentation of Tithes and Offerings

In calling Moses, the Lord promised to be with him, and in calling us, God promises the church no less. As Moses was given a specific task in his day, so God has a mission and a purpose for the church today, a purpose that invites us to offer our best service. Let us render our gifts to God.

Prayer of Dedication

None of us truly lives until we live in you, O God. None of us gives in faith, unless we give in the name of Jesus. None of our gifts can bring life or liberty unless they are given with love, the love of your holiness. Make these gifts holy, we pray; make our hearts pure and our lives bright, burning reflections of your Spirit within us.

The Blessing

The fire of the Spirit is the light that never dies.
The light of the world is the Christ of the cross.
The cross of Christ reveals the long-suffering love of God.
Take them with you as you go.

Proper 18
Ordinary Time 23 / September 4–10

Exodus 12:1–14
Psalm 149
Romans 13:8–14
Matthew 18:15–20

IN PREPARATION FOR WORSHIP

Gracious God, we remember with joy your promise
to be with us wherever two or three gather in your name.
Mindful of your steadfast love and faithfulness, we assemble once again,
that you might hear our songs in praise of your righteousness,
act on our prayers in deference to your will,
and receive our thanksgiving
for your saving grace.

CALL TO WORSHIP

Put on the Lord Jesus Christ!
For now is the moment to awake from slumber.
> We make ready for the journey from death to life eternal.
> For the blood of the Lamb has spared us from the plague of death.

Sing to our victorious God!
Offer the living LORD the symphony of your hearts.
> Our common ground is our risen Lord,
> who has purchased our salvation.

Opening Prayer

God of the Passover, in your covenant, you have saved and elected a holy people and appointed them to service. We thank you that in your freedom you have chosen to be gracious, and we are humbled that you have elected us in Christ to be your loving, reconciling people. Strengthen us to resist every temptation, and prepare us for grateful discipleship, for the integrity of your church and for the glory of your name.

Call to Confession

The power of sin is a real fact of life. The creation is broken, and the evil that is present in the world has fatally compromised our human nature and infected every human heart. Yet, by God's gracious plan for our redemption, the blood of Christ cleanses us from sin, and we are able to lay aside the works of darkness and put on the armor of light. The wonderful promise is that when we ask for forgiveness, we receive it. Let us confess our sin to God.

Prayer of Confession

Freeing and forgiving God, we declare your rightness in judging sinful deeds wrong, and we confess our failure to fulfill your righteous commandments. We have rebelled against you and retreated from your costly ways of love. Redirect our wandering feet, purify our wayward hearts, and humble our proud thoughts. Forgive our guilt and sin, that we might serve you with renewed resolve and labor for the glory of your merciful and gracious Son, in whose name we pray.

Declaration of Forgiveness

Jesus is called the Lamb of God for this reason: his blood has secured our salvation, just as the blood of the Passover lamb saved Israel from the angel of death. In this new covenant, sealed in the blood of Christ, we are set free from sin's tyranny and from the punishment for sin, which is death. Forgiveness is ours in our new covenant with Christ.

Presentation of Tithes and Offerings

Praise the Lord! Let the whole assembly of the faithful exult in the glory of God. Be glad in your Maker, who adorns the humble with victory. Let us offer our gifts in praise of Christ our Savior!

Prayer of Dedication

O God, our great benefactor, these gifts are yours, to be used as you direct and inspire us. We thank you for entrusting them to us. As we return them to you, may they be to us as seeds that die in the ground, and to you as the means of a fruitful and bountiful harvest of love.

The Blessing

The Lord has called you from sin to freedom.
Christ has called you to live in peace.
Go, therefore, in the power of the Spirit,
to bear the fruit of a blessed life,
giving glory and honor and thanks to God
in all that you say and do.

Proper 19
Ordinary Time 24 / September 11–17

Exodus 14:19–31

Psalm 114 OR Exodus 15:1b–11

Romans 14:1–12

Matthew 18:21–35

IN PREPARATION FOR WORSHIP

O God of power and mercy,
what great deeds you have done!
You have parted the waters for your people.
You have paid the unpayable debt that we owed.
You have promised us life on the other side of death.
May we worthily exalt you in this hour,
for you have used your power
to show us the greatest mercy.

CALL TO WORSHIP

Come, Almighty Father.
    Bathe us in the knowledge of your presence.
Come, merciful Christ.
    Those you have saved give thanks for your grace.
Come, Spirit of Life.
    Fill our hearts with compassion.

Come, triune God!
> We are gathered in your name.

Opening Prayer

God of compassion and grace, who alone reverses the capital sentence, who alone reconciles the infinite debt, grant us an audience, we pray, that we might know in the depths of our being your unending love, your almighty mercy, and that we might bear witness to it in the life of your church, for the sake of Christ's mission in the world.

Call to Confession

In confession, we recognize our incalculable debt to God, and all that we have in common with the fallen human race. The greatest debts we owe one another are nothing compared to our indebtedness to God. Let us appeal, therefore, to the one who, by his death on the cross, has demonstrated God's infinite love and perfect human obedience. Mindful of God's steadfast love, let us confess our sin.

Prayer of Confession

Forgiving God, who has promised to liberate us for new life: Egypt is behind us and the sea is before us! Despite our doubts, our fears, and our memories of past sins, forgive us and part the waters. Lead us through the waters of regeneration, see us safely to the other side, that we might emerge, cleansed and restored, into the new life and the holy calling for which you have elected your people. We ask this in Jesus' name.

Declaration of Forgiveness

When asked if one should forgive as many as seven times, Jesus multiplied this answer many times over. In this we have our assurance. Perfect forgiveness involves no scorekeeping, but a continual regimen of relentless surrender. We know this because Christ, who forgives perfectly, surrendered everything, that we might know we are forgiven in him.

Presentation of Tithes and Offerings

What we do to others, we do to ourselves; but when we bless others, something similar, and often far greater, is done for us by God. We reap what we sow. Therefore, let us scatter the seeds of God's grace with generosity and good cheer, confident of a bountiful harvest. Let us thank God by giving, as God does, from the heart.

Prayer of Dedication

You are a God who hears the cries of the suffering, who turns the sea into solid, dry ground and buries the hostile enemy. You alone can give a glorious answer to our humblest prayers and turn our most dire circumstances into opportunities for fruitfulness and joy. Take these humble gifts, we pray, and turn them into something great, for the furtherance of your holy kingdom and for the glory of your holy name.

The Blessing

Let your hearts be filled with the joy of the Spirit.
Let your minds be inspired by God's sheer, saving grace.
Let your walk be unburdened in the freedom of Christ.
And may you always be grateful and quick to forgive.

Proper 20
Ordinary Time 25 / September 18–24

Exodus 16:2–15
Psalm 105:1–6, 37–45
Philippians 1:21–30
Matthew 20:1–16

In Preparation for Worship

Holy God, you give freely and yet with a purpose.
You provide the worthy goal and the means to reach it.
You not only hire unworthy workers,
you bear fruit through our imperfect work.
By the power of your Spirit, recall us to our reason for being
and remind us what it means that we are yours.

Call to Worship

Be not anxious what your wages shall be,
but come and labor in the vineyard of God.
>   **Whether we are late or early,**
>   **our Lord is both generous and fair.**

Worry not about what you will eat,
but come receive manna from the hand of God.
>   **Let us worship the God of the covenant,**
>   **who both knows our needs and provides.**

Opening Prayer

God of grace, who grants us meaningful work, ample provision, and the assurance of a life beyond this life, we approach you in faith, seeking your face, your Word, and your guiding Spirit, that our labors might bring joy to your people, and our lives might be lived in a manner worthy of the gospel of Christ.

Call to Confession

How often have we compared ourselves to others, judging ourselves against the successes and shortcomings of our neighbors! Surely it is sinful to tear others down, just as it is to build ourselves up at their expense. But the measure we give is the measure we get. Let us confess the inequity in our lives, and in our vision of others, revealing our sin to God, our most gracious and forgiving judge.

Prayer of Confession

O God, you are the source of all our blessings. Yet we confess that we have often complained of the unfairness of life. We harbor envy and discontentment, and we fail to consider what you would have us learn in every circumstance. Forgive us for our many sins and our moments of ingratitude. Transform our complaint into delight, our downcast eyes into brightly shining lamps, lit with the living flame of the Spirit of Jesus Christ, in whose name we pray.

Declaration of Forgiveness

Those who are arrogant are forgetful of past sins; they will soon be humbled. But those who remember their sins humble themselves, and Christ in turn lifts them up. This is, in part, why Jesus said, "The last shall be first, and the first shall be last." Having humbly confessed, now be reassured that in Jesus Christ you are forgiven.

Presentation of Tithes and Offerings

As God sends abundant bread from heaven, as the landlord deals generously with those hired late, let us likewise gather our offerings, with joy in the act of giving and with one mind in the life of Christ.

Prayer of Dedication

By your free will and gracious hand, we have these treasures to share.
By your open hand and generous heart, we have these hearts to devote to you.
By your loving heart and living sacrifice, we have these lives to live for you.
Accept them as your own, and do with them what you would have us do.

The Blessing

Stand firm in the one Spirit and work with one purpose: the glory of God.
Live in a worthy manner and your labor will bear an eternal reward.
For your living is Christ and your dying is gain.

Proper 21
Ordinary Time 26 / September 25–October 1

Exodus 17:1–7
Psalm 78:1–4, 12–16
Philippians 2:1–13
Matthew 21:23–32

IN PREPARATION FOR WORSHIP

O the depths to which you have lowered yourself,
that you might lift us up!
Your Son has delivered us, as a servant from heaven sent to save.
Your Spirit fills and satisfies, like water from a desert rock.
Fill us anew, we pray, with the knowledge of your presence,
that we might extol you and be empowered to serve you
throughout the world.

CALL TO WORSHIP

Gather, O people. Lift up the name of Jesus.
>   We confess him the living Lord of all,
>   who has raised us from death to life!

Consider the glorious deeds of the LORD.
>   Let us teach God's wondrous deeds to the next generation.

Encourage one another in Christ, that your joy might be complete.
>   We will share the knowledge of God in the Holy Spirit of love.
>   Let us worship God.

Opening Prayer

O Lord Most High, you are above and beneath, before and beyond, all that we can comprehend. Meet us here, in this time and place, amidst this gathering, that your presence in and among your chosen people might be seen and known through all the world, in Jesus' name.

Call to Confession

The power of sin is expressed in many forms. But the same God who condemns sin in all its forms has gone to incomprehensible extremes to save sinners through Christ Jesus, "who, though he was in the form of God, did not regard equality with God as something to be exploited, but emptied himself, taking the form of a slave, being born in human likeness. And being found in human form, he humbled himself and became obedient to the point of death, even death on a cross." When we confess, we not only admit our sin, we also testify that Jesus Christ saves sinners. Let us do so together.

Prayer of Confession

You are a God who both leads and brings up the rear. Yet at times we would race ahead in zeal, presuming to show ourselves worthy; at other times, we lag behind, wondering what we have to offer, doubting even that we can be saved. Steady us, O Lord. Shepherd us onto the straight path. Forgive our rebellious judgments and our self-centered despair. Help us to trust in your saving grace and to recommit ourselves to following the example set for us in Jesus Christ our Lord.

Declaration of Forgiveness

God is at work in you! Jesus Christ, who has the authority to forgive sins, authorizes us to forgive one another. The Holy Spirit renews us for life in the vast grace of God. Hear, believe, and live according to this good news: in Jesus Christ, you are forgiven!

Presentation of Tithes and Offerings

Bring the baskets! Distribute the plates! Pass them among you, and give to the Lord!

Prayer of Dedication

You have secured our salvation with no army of your own. You have purchased our redemption with no money to your name. You author a new creation with little more than a word. To such a mighty work as is your ministry of Word and Spirit, we, your servant people, dedicate these gifts. May they serve to glorify your holy name.

The Blessing

One son said, "I will do it," and did not.
One son said, "I will not," yet did.
As for you, go in the Spirit of Jesus Christ,
who said, "Thy will be done," then suffered it.
Go in peace to love and serve the Lord.

Proper 22
Ordinary Time 27 / October 2–8

Exodus 20:1–4, 7–9, 12–20
Psalm 19
Philippians 3:4b–14
Matthew 21:33–46

IN PREPARATION FOR WORSHIP

Come, Abba, Father, God of the mountain;
come, Word of God, Lord of all life;
come, holy wind and flame, life of the church:
your people are gathered, in great need of grace.

CALL TO WORSHIP

Tell the world of the glory of the LORD:
> **The glory of God is a rejected glory.**
> **Yet, the stone the builders rejected has become our cornerstone.**

Our cornerstone is Christ:
> **To know him and the power of his resurrection**
> **surpasses everything of value.**

Know the rejected Son, and build your lives upon him:
> **For Christ has made us his own;**
> **therefore, let us press on undaunted**
> **toward our heavenly call in Christ Jesus.**

Opening Prayer

Holy Lord, in your covenant, you have given us both law and grace; as your Word stands watch over our often wayward lives, your mercy surrounds us. Gather us anew in the name of your Son Jesus Christ, that we might learn from his passion and goodness, obedience and faith, reverence and love, and that your promises might come to fruition in our lives, in this generation.

Call to Confession

The ten commandments of God are unqualified. They demand that we give our ultimate loyalty, faith, and obedience to God. No one is above the law. Everyone has sinned and fallen short of its standard. Therefore, let us confess and renounce the power of sin in our lives, in the life of the church, and in the whole sphere of human relations.

Prayer of Confession

Holy God, your gift of the law is an act of grace, a penetrating light exposing the temptations of this world. In its light we see how we have violated your commandments and sought to conceal our sin beneath mounds of good deeds that, nevertheless, remain overshadowed by Sinai. Forgive our pretense to perfection, hear our confession of sin, and raise us to new life, freed from the law by the death of Christ, freed to walk with him in the abundant joy of your eternal realm.

Declaration of Forgiveness

The fear of God may keep one from sinning. But we have sinned, and when we confess it, Christ forgives us by the power of his gracious love. So shall we love or fear God? The greatest commandment is to love God and neighbor, but to love God with reverent fear is best of all. Therefore, as God's forgiven people, let the fear of God keep you from sin. But let the love of God guide you in the service of his love.

Presentation of Tithes and Offerings

As Christ has given everything for us, even his body and his blood, so we should give of our deepest substance, as deep as our very hearts and minds, to find suitable offerings for our Lord. In the light of Christ's presence with us, let us render unto God the offerings of our lives and the fruits of our labor in God's own vineyard.

Prayer of Dedication

Ever-gracious and holy Word of God, use these gifts as you desire. No gift can match what you have given for us. Therefore, receive these offerings along with our love, for only with love may we offer them worthily.

The Blessing

Do not claim that you know all about Christ.
Seek to know him, even as he has claimed you for his own.
Do not claim for yourselves righteous obedience to the law.
Seek to live in the grace of our Lord.
Do not claim to have the Spirit of God at your disposal.
Seek to live your life in the service of the Spirit.
And may God bless you and keep you as you go.

Proper 23
Ordinary Time 28 / October 9–15

Exodus 32:1–14
Psalm 106:1–6, 19–23
Philippians 4:1–9
Matthew 22:1–14

In Preparation for Worship

Lord, yours is the peace
that passes all understanding.
Yours is the truth, the majesty,
the righteousness, the purity of spirit.
As we gather to worship you, turn our minds to think
on such holy things as are unsurpassably met in you.

Call to Worship

The world fashions many idols.
> **There is but one Lord of heaven and earth.**

Many are called . . .
> **but few are chosen.**

Let those whom God has called be sanctified and made ready to worship.
> **We lift our hearts to God, in love, devotion, and joy.**

Opening Prayer

Our gracious Host, you have invited us to the wedding banquet of your Son, our Savior Jesus Christ. Help us put aside all lesser invitations and obligations, so that we may ready ourselves to receive him as the worthy bridegroom and to be received as his guests; we ask this in Jesus' name.

Call to Confession

Just as we prepare to attend a wedding in our best attire, so we must also ready ourselves to attend Christ's wedding celebration. Such preparation warrants the utmost seriousness, yet should also inspire our eager anticipation of good things to come, for indeed this is how the Spirit prepares us when we confess our sins, ask God's forgiveness, and wash our garments in the blood of Christ.

Prayer of Confession

Merciful God, no sooner did you give your law to Moses than Israel engaged in idol worship. No sooner do you forgive us than we return to the destructive habits of sin, mold our treasures into golden calves, and codify our talents into lifeless routines. Forgive us, we pray, for we know you are a forgiving God, having forgiven the sins of previous generations. Preserve us and reform us for willing and faithful obedience, that the world may know us by our love for and our obedience to you, in the name of Jesus, our high priest and mediator.

Declaration of Forgiveness

The beauty of forgiveness lies in its power to set us free. True freedom comes not from within us; it is a gift from God in Christ Jesus, who alone has the power to condemn but who steadfastly chooses to love us instead, and to endure human sin, until we learn the better way. Let us resolve to learn the paths of righteousness in which our divine Shepherd leads us. It is by walking these paths, following Christ's lead, that we find true freedom.

Presentation of Tithes and Offerings

Bring your gifts to the Lord, for Jesus Christ will soon be wedded to his church. Give from the heart, with the joy of knowing what it means to love and to be loved. Ready yourselves for the celebration to which all have been invited, at which you, the church, shall be the bride of Christ. For what you give as a guest you will receive as the beloved of God on the wedding day of our Lord.

Prayer of Dedication

Lord Jesus, you have called us to be your people, your guests, your nuptial community. We offer you these gifts, as servants to their sovereign, as a wife to her husband, praying for their purity and usefulness, that they might bring you honor and demonstrate our reverence and love for you, in the grace of your Holy Spirit.

The Blessing

As many of you as have ever worshipped God, put away every idol.
As many of you as have ever loved, ready yourselves for the wedding feast.
As many of you as have ever felt the stirrings of the Spirit,
submit your lives to the triune God.
For surely, when it comes to making the most of the time,
you can do nothing so good as this.

Proper 24
Ordinary Time 29 / October 16–22

Exodus 33:12–23

Psalm 99

1 Thessalonians 1:1–10

Matthew 22:15–22

In Preparation for Worship

Our holy and living God,
may your name be exalted;
may your glory be increased;
may your presence be known in our presence
as we gather to render you thanks, honor, and adoration.

Call to Worship

Let the Word of the Lord sound forth.
> **May the Word be heard by all**
> **who are made in the image of God.**

The Lord is holy and mighty.
> **Let us forsake every idol**
> **and worship the one living and true God.**

Give to all the honor that is due them.
> **Above all, give to God what belongs to God:**
> **your heart, soul, strength, and mind,**
> **your lives of service and devout worship.**

Opening Prayer

As Moses conferred with you on Mount Sinai, and dared to ask to see you; as you allowed your glory to pass by him, protecting him with your hand and sheltering him from your face, we ask your intimate presence with us, not presuming to be holy in and of ourselves, yet desiring to draw near to your holiness in humility and faith. Come, holy God!

Call to Confession

While we, in our sin, are prohibited from seeing the face of our holy God, Scripture also tells us to seek God's face, since we are created in the divine image. This image, marred by human iniquity, is nevertheless restored by Christ. Therefore, if we are to seek God's face, we are to seek it in the person of Jesus. Let us appeal to God through Christ, confessing our sin, that God's image in us might be made new again.

Prayer of Confession

God of creation, your power and majesty are greater than all our imaginings. You form the atoms we cannot see, you scatter the stars across infinite space, and you fashion us to be like you. Yet we fail you again and again, disobeying your commands, indulging hidden desires, and forgetting the dignity with which you would have us treat one another, the kindness you would have us show one another. Forgive us, O God, and restore your hidden glory within us, through the grace of Jesus Christ our redeemer.

Declaration of Forgiveness

Christ is seated at the right hand of God, the very hand with which God protected Moses from the Lord's unveiled goodness. Christ is not only seated at the right hand of power, at one with God in goodness and mercy, but as the fully human Christ, he imparts to us the renewed image of God of which he himself is the pattern and prototype. Friends, know that in Jesus Christ you are forgiven, and be at peace.

Presentation of Tithes and Offerings

It is our duty and responsibility to render to the civil authorities what is due them. Even Jesus Christ did the same, offering a coin taken from the mouth of a fish, and ultimately submitting to the sentence of death, unjust though it was. But we answer the call of God when we return what belongs to God. For while the coin was forcefully stamped in the image of Caesar, we are lovingly made in the image of God, who has given us everything, including his beloved Son Jesus Christ, for our salvation and restoration. Let us lovingly return what is due to God, for Jesus Christ has already claimed us.

Prayer of Dedication

As you have made human beings in your divine image, we offer you ourselves, that through us you might reveal your holiness to the world, despite our flaws and imperfections. We thank you for the restoring work of Christ our Redeemer, in whose name we offer this currency in good faith, trusting that your Spirit of charity will increase it for the benefit of those in need, and that all that is rightfully yours might return to you, the Source of all life.

The Blessing

Honor God's image in those whom you meet.
Serve the Christ in whom you are made new.
Invite the Holy Spirit into every situation,
and you shall see the coming of Christ!

Proper 25
Ordinary Time 30 / October 23–29

Deuteronomy 34:1–12
Psalm 90:1–6, 13–17
1 Thessalonians 2:1–8
Matthew 22:34–46

IN PREPARATION FOR WORSHIP

God Most High, you are the author of the covenant;
Christ of Righteousness, you are our high priest forever;
Spirit of Wisdom, you are our guide to the promised land.
Fill us with such grace and love that it may be said that we,
your church, obey your great commands.

CALL TO WORSHIP

The greatest commandment is to love the Lord your God
with all your heart, all your soul, and all your mind.
>   The second is like it:
>   We shall love our neighbors as we love ourselves.
These two commandments support all the law and the words of the prophets.
>   Love subdues the enemies of Christ.
Indeed, God has said to Jesus Christ,
>   "Sit at my right hand, until I put your enemies under your feet."

Opening Prayer

Living God, your almighty mercy is such that you transform law into promise, raise obedience into joy, and turn commandments into works of love. We thank you that your law gives us guidance and directs us toward you, and that your Spirit inspires and propels us along our earthly way toward your kingdom. We praise you that when we meet you, we need not rely on our merit to enter, but on the grace with which you receive us in the person of Jesus Christ.

Call to Confession

The law will only get us so far—and we fall short of it anyway. But when we confess our sin, we confess not only our breaking of the law, our inability to obey it; we also confess our need for something, and someone, greater than the law. That something is grace, that someone is Christ. Let us confess both our sin and our need for Christ.

Prayer of Confession

God of love, we confess that we have reduced your commands to empty rules. Too rarely do we take the high road of loving, and even then, the best love we can offer, to you and to others, is a partial love. Be gracious to us; in your mercy hear us. Increase within us our capacity and our eagerness to know, to show, and to share your love according to the abundant measure with which you bless us, in Jesus' name.

Declaration of Forgiveness

Christ surpasses Moses and Elijah in prophecy. Christ excels Aaron and Levi as our high priest. Christ is a priest forever in the order of Melchizedek, King of Righteousness, fulfilling God's law for us, offering himself as a sacrifice for our sin, and raising us to new life with him in the glory of his resurrection. This is why Christ has come and will come again, that we might trust and live by these words: in Jesus Christ, we are forgiven.

Presentation of Tithes and Offerings

Christ tells us that our love for God should be total, filling our hearts entirely, instructing our minds completely, and inspiring our intentions. This is how and why our act of giving is fruitful, practical, and thus basic to the Christian life. When we give our offerings to God, we clear away that which would disrupt the flow of love between us and God. If we withhold from God our material gifts, we will also surely withhold our love. But if we free ourselves of all that would come between us and God, we set ourselves free to love God and one another more fully.

Prayer of Dedication

Love flows from your very essence, O God. Yet love is something we must learn. Grace arises from your very heart, O Christ. Yet we often think grace is to be earned. Life is a gift from your very Spirit, O Holy One. Yet life is limited by our fear. Give life to these gifts, O Blessed Trinity, these gifts made ours by your grace, made yours again in love, in Jesus' name.

The Blessing

Take the gospel into your hearts,
and may your life show the world that you love God fully.
Share the gospel with one another,
and may the Spirit flow from neighbor to neighbor.
Tell the gospel to the world,
and may your witness to God's love lead others to Christ,
as Jesus sets you free to love.

Proper 26
Ordinary Time 31 / October 30–November 5

Joshua 3:7–17

Psalm 107:1–7, 33–37

1 Thessalonians 2:9–13

Matthew 23:1–12

In Preparation for Worship

O Lord our God,
we have but one Lord, in heaven;
we have but one teacher, the Christ;
we have but one instructor, the Spirit of counsel,
and we are all brothers and sisters.
We humbly worship you,
waiting upon you,
to do your will.

Call to Worship

Gather, O people, for the Lord is with us.
> **God makes a sure path for us through flowing waters.**

Gather, O people, and prepare yourselves.
> **Pride is laid low, humility is exalted.**

Gather, O people, and place your trust in the Lord.
> **God's promise of land is a sure promise
> where we are free to serve.**

Opening Prayer

High and holy God, as your covenantal ark was carried across the flooding river Jordan at harvest-time, you made the water stop its flow and Israel to pass safely through the river on dry land. Lead us, O God, as Noah through the flood, as Israel at the Red Sea, as souls whom you baptize with your Holy Spirit; lead us through to the land of promise. Lead us, O Christ. We will follow. We will trust.

Call to Confession

Holiness is not possible without confession of sin. Confession serves not to embarrass or to burden anyone with guilt. It serves only to acknowledge God's perfect goodness and to set us free to receive the gift of holiness that is given to all who sincerely humble themselves. Let us confess our sin.

Prayer of Confession

God of creation, your power and greatness are such that the very feet of the priests, who held your holy seat aloft in the Jordan, dispelled the waters. Yet we, in our day, are more like the priests, the teachers, and the Pharisees about whom Jesus warned his disciples: saying one thing and doing another; seeking honor for ourselves at the expense of others; forgetting and forsaking the stewardship of humble service. Forgive us, O God. We have sinned, and we need your help to find the right way: the way of justice, kindness, and humility.

Declaration of Forgiveness

Jesus said, "All who exalt themselves will be humbled." But he also said, "All who humble themselves will be exalted." Sinners who admit their sins honestly are justified before those who merely adorn themselves with outward signs of holiness, those who remain inwardly proud, even of their humility. Humble sinners, God has heard your confession. God lifts you up. For in Jesus Christ, you are forgiven.

Presentation of Tithes and Offerings

There is never a time when thanksgiving is inappropriate. Thanks should ever be our first and our last word to God. Gratitude is the defining characteristic of the Christian life, and giving is the natural response, the instinctive impulse of those who have been saved by the grace of God. Let us gratefully offer our gifts to God.

Prayer of Dedication

Giver of all good gifts, we thank you that you have accompanied us through the high waters to this harvesttime, and into a season of plenty. We are humbled by your immeasurable goodness to us. We offer you these gifts from our first fruits, from the abundance you have given, even as we begin to consider new ways in which we might give, all for the sake of your glory, for the glory of your risen Son, and for the life of the Spirit. Triune God, we pray, give life to these your gifts.

The Blessing

God humbles the proud and lifts up the lowly, so walk humbly with him. Christ teaches the teacher as well as the student, so learn well from the master. The Spirit tests the hearts of all the people of God, so let your hearts be guided in the way of grace, gratitude, and peace.

All Saints' Day
November 1 (or *First Sunday in November*)

Revelation 7:9–17
Psalm 34:1–10, 22
1 John 3:1–3
Matthew 5:1–12

In Preparation for Worship

I seek your face, O Lord my God.
I look to you that I may shine.
I search for you, Eternal Word,
for heaven's bread, the Spirit's wine.
I bless you, Lord; I boast of you.
I sing, with the heavenly hosts, of you,
for you raise the dead, you save the lost,
you satisfy our every thirst
with the clear, bright, pure, and shining
water of life!

Call to Worship

Come, wash and be clean.
Make your garments white in the blood of the Lamb.
> "Salvation belongs to our God
> who is seated on the throne, and to the Lamb!"

All Saints' Day—November 1

Come, take your place before the throne of God.
Worship the Lord day and night in God's holy temple.
> "Amen! Blessing and praise and glory and wisdom,
> thanksgiving and honor and power and might
> be unto our God forever and ever! Amen!"

Come, take shelter in the Holy One.
The Lamb of God will be our shepherd and guide us to the water of life!
> **The Lord will redeem the life of the faithful.**
> **God shall wipe away every tear.**

Opening Prayer

Loving God, who dignifies sinners by adopting them as children, we await the revealing of your glory; we hope in your holy purity, for we know that when your Beloved is revealed, our Savior and Lord, we will be like him. Therefore, we gather in the hope that we will be purified for that final day.

Call to Confession

God has seen fit to provide us a deliverer, to save us from every trouble, and to purchase our freedom from every sin. Those who take refuge in God are truly happy, for they know the blessed joy of having the Lord for their God, their sovereign protector. Therefore, let those who fear the Lord draw near and confess their need for forgiveness and salvation.

Prayer of Confession

Holy God, you know better than anyone the ordeals we suffer, as well as those that we instigate and to which we contribute. We admit that the things you call blessed make us uneasy. We fear poverty, grief, meekness, hunger, and thirst. Yet we often go so far to avoid them that we miss entirely your good intentions for our growth, joy, integrity, and peace of mind. Forgive us, Lord, for being so shortsighted. Cleanse us from every sin and stain. Free us from our fears. Make us bold to witness to your love.

Declaration of Forgiveness

Let the humble hear and be glad and make their boast in the Lord: No one who takes refuge in God will be condemned, for the Lord redeems the humble. Those who seek the Lord lack no good thing. Look to God and be radiant, and you need never be ashamed. Let us bless the Lord at all times, who has, through Christ, forgiven all our sins!

Presentation of Tithes and Offerings

Let the children of God have every confidence in God's goodness and love. Those who fear and revere the Lord shall suffer no want or deprivation. The meek and the lowly, the humble and the worshipful shall inherit the earth and all of God's rich blessings with it. Theirs shall be the kingdom of heaven. Therefore, let all who would live under the rule of God's sovereign love offer tribute with thanksgiving and joy and praise!

Prayer of Dedication

Holy One, we claim no property that you have not provided. We claim no happiness that you have not inspired. We are poor in spirit, poor in merit, poor in good deeds. You are our only true wealth and blessing, our only true hope, our reason for rejoicing! Therefore, we submit all to you, with these humble tokens of tribute as signs of your sovereignty over our lives. Bless them, we pray, that in their use the glory of your governance might be seen at home and abroad!

The Blessing

May every corner of your life: every thought and affection,
every word, every action,
be ordered by the kingdom of heaven and blessed for your joy
by our triune God!

Proper 27
Ordinary Time 32 / November 6–12

Joshua 24:1–3a, 14–25

Psalm 78:1–7

1 Thessalonians 4:13–18

Matthew 25:1–13

In Preparation for Worship

Creating and Liberating God,
you have graced us with freedom to choose whom we will serve,
and you have promised to return and gather the faithful to yourself.
Know that in this hour, we choose you anew for our God.
Grant us courage and strength of faith to hold fast to your covenant
in the time that remains to us, until you come again.

Call to Worship

Come, O people, and declare the mighty deeds of the Lord.
    The Lord has saved us! Let us tell it to our children.
Come, O people, and choose this day whom you will serve.
    "As for me and my house, we will serve the Lord!"
Come, O people, and teach the young what God has done once and for all.
    Christ has died for us! Christ is risen!
    Christ will come again to meet us and to gather us home.

Opening Prayer

Eternal and ever-gracious God, your deeds are recorded deep in the memory of your chosen people. May your Holy Spirit make us bold and give us the words, the deeds, the acts of faith and stewardship, to share the good news of our coming Redeemer with all the living generations, for your glory and for their salvation, in Jesus' name.

Call to Confession

When the people of Israel swore an oath to serve the LORD, Joshua told them, "You are witnesses against yourselves that you have chosen the LORD, to serve him." And they said, "We are witnesses." Then Joshua erected a large stone under an oak tree, and he said, "See, this stone shall be a witness against us, for it has heard all the words of the LORD that he spoke to us; therefore it shall be a witness against you, if you deal falsely with your God." All of us must face such reminders of how we have sinned against God and neighbor. Let us confess our sin to God, and in full view of one another, mindful that we too are witnesses to the false motives that have driven us in the past.

Prayer of Confession

Saving God, you call us to total obedience and loyalty, faith, and love. Yet we confess to you that our houses and our hearts are not free of idols. Illumine the dark corners of our cowardice and sin, so that we may no longer fear what the shadows hide. Forgive us, and help us put both house and heart in order. Where the tried is indeed true, help us remain faithful to the truth. And where the untried is truer still, give us courage to step into the light of total obedience to your will, for the sake of our saving Christ.

Declaration of Forgiveness

We have all labored under the burden of sin. Nevertheless, in Jesus Christ, God remakes human beings so that we now have the potential to remain alert, to resist sin, and to replace it with good works of fruitful obedience. The beauty of God's grace is that, in choosing not to condemn us for our sins, we are given one opportunity after another, not so much to get it right the next time, but to turn our lives over to God and to allow the obedient life of Jesus Christ to unfold within us. Friends, know that you are not condemned. You are forgiven! Now welcome your gracious Lord into the open spaces left vacant by sin.

Presentation of Tithes and Offerings

As we have chosen this day to serve the Lord, let us demonstrate our faith by entrusting our gifts to God, praying that they might be multiplied for the glory of the heavenly kingdom that Jesus Christ has gone ahead to prepare for us. For, as the Lord said, "Where your treasure is, there will your heart be also."

Prayer of Dedication

From our first fruits we dedicate to you this portion of the blessings you have granted us. May they bear witness to our faith in and love for you, as they also testify to the gracious goodness that has come to us in the person of your Son and our Savior, Christ Jesus.

The Blessing

The choice must be made every day; let us forever resolve to serve the Lord. The bridegroom may come at any time; therefore, keep awake, alert, and alive. Christ shall return to reunite us with all the saints; therefore, wait and hope and trust in the Lord.

Proper 28
Ordinary Time 33 / November 13–19

Judges 4:1–7
Psalm 123
1 Thessalonians 5:1–11
Matthew 25:14–30

In Preparation for Worship

Giver of all good gifts,
in whom alone we trust for eternal salvation,
make us expectant and ready to receive you,
to render an accounting of all you have given us,
and make us hopeful of being received
when you come again.

Call to Worship

Search the heavens for the mercy of God.
> As servants look to their master,
> we will look to the Lord.

Search the horizons for the coming of Christ.
> As servants desire to please their master,
> we will seek to please the Lord.

Search your lives for the gifts of the Spirit.
> As servants wait upon the word of the Lord,
> we will serve and hope to hear the words,
> "Well done, good and faithful servant."

Opening Prayer

Gracious Master, you have entrusted to us what is yours: not merely money, but talents and interests, skills and knowledge, goals and gifts, health and harmony. Stir our memories, our imaginations, and our forgotten dreams of neglected gifts, that we might grow and develop them all to your purpose, your glory, and your good pleasure.

Call to Confession

We are more gifted, more blessed, and more accountable for our blessings than we realize. When we recognize that everything in our lives, even every trial and every loss, is somehow a grace, then we are confronted with the worst of all sins: ingratitude. How often have we, like the wicked and lazy servant, misjudged the Lord to be harsh, reaping where God has not sown? How often have we mistrusted what has been sown in us? Let us confess our sin.

Prayer of Confession

Living, loving Lord, we know that we should first trust that your love for us is behind every gift and every challenge that comes our way. You know, better than we do, what is best for us. Yet our instinct is not to trust but to fear you, to hide from your judgments, and to hoard what we might lose. Forgive and reform us, remake us in the image of Jesus Christ, who is your image and who, as your Son, withholds nothing from you.

Declaration of Forgiveness

The assurance of Scripture is that God has not destined us for wrath, but for obtaining salvation through our Lord Jesus Christ. It is not only our will, but it is God's will and the will of Jesus Christ, the eternal Word, that we should be saved; and the Word of the Lord will not return to God empty. Friends, it is by the gracious goodness of our saving Lord that we are forgiven. Trust that this is true, and be at peace.

Presentation of Tithes and Offerings

Salvation is not the chief purpose of our lives; it is rather the means to a greater end: the glory of God and our complete joy in God's presence. It is toward this end that we cultivate our God-given gifts. By allowing the Spirit of Christ to take root in our lives, we shall produce a fruitful yield, pleasing to God. The Spirit of Christ is a giving Spirit. Let us therefore be both inspired and disciplined in our giving, knowing that that our gifts will bear good fruit to the delight and the glory of God.

Prayer of Dedication

To you we owe all our gifts, O Lord, all our gratitude, all our love. Of all that you have given us, we set these gifts apart, and offer you our humble prayers that they might increase, produce a harvest, and yield good fruit worthy of your Spirit, who alone can bring them to life, in Jesus' name.

The Blessing

May the blessings of our Creator God,
the grace of the Redeeming Christ,
the fruits of the Holy Spirit of Life,
be alive and active in you,
that you may one day be welcomed
into the kingdom of heaven with the words,
"Well done, good and faithful servant."

Proper 29
Ordinary Time 34 / November 20–26
(Christ the King or Reign of Christ)

Ezekiel 34:11–16, 20–24

Psalm 100

Ephesians 1:15–23

Matthew 25:31–46

In Preparation for Worship

The world has many rulers, but you are our God:
you, O God of Israel.
The powers of the world compete for control,
but you make power perfect in weakness:
you, the crucified and risen Lord.
The world knows many spirits,
but you are our hope and our enlightenment:
you, the Spirit of wisdom and revelation.
We come to glorify you and give you thanks!

Call to Worship

You, O Lord, are God of heaven and earth.
    You, O Christ, are the good shepherd of the people.
You, O Holy Spirit, reveal truth where there is compassion.
    Your kingdom shall come as you rule over our lives.

It is here! The reign of God is here!
We enter your gates with thanksgiving, your gates with praise!

Opening Prayer

Almighty God, from a holy conception you came to us, an infant; from humble beginnings, you grew among your people; in the synagogues of Israel, you proclaimed the good news of God's reign on earth; from the cross you were lowered and buried, having suffered for our sin; and from your grave you were raised anew, all to show us the goodness of God. Who is worthy to be our Lord and God, our hope and our salvation, but you, O Christ the King, Son of the Most High God!

Call to Confession

Jesus tells us that when we help one in need, we help him. But whenever we neglect one in need, we neglect him as well. In the coming kingdom of heaven, we shall treat our sisters and brothers as royalty, as we should treat Christ himself. Let us appeal to the mercy of God for failing to serve Jesus Christ and our neighbors as we should.

Prayer of Confession

Ever-present God, you have witnessed and felt firsthand our every act of abuse, neglect, and rebuff. We have often gone our own way, rather than help the least of our sisters and brothers in Christ. In your mercy, forgive us. Help us to see you in all whom we meet, regardless of their circumstances, and to serve them as eagerly as we would fall at your feet.

Declaration of Forgiveness

Open your eyes to see; unplug your ears to hear; unveil your hearts to receive the good news. The steadfast love and mercy of the Lord endure forever. Like the eternal Word of God, the eternal Son reigns supreme, a good shepherd. God will single-handedly bind up where wickedness has injured, will seek and bring back those who have strayed, will strengthen the weak and feed the hungry. In the kingdom of God, Christ rules with mercy. Know that you are forgiven, live with one another in love, and be at peace in your hearts.

Presentation of Tithes and Offerings

Knowing that the Lord Jesus Christ is all around you, and alive in our very midst, what will you offer in thanksgiving?

Prayer of Dedication

God of compassion and truth, the blessings that come from knowing you are innumerable and amazing. The offerings we make with contrite hearts we know you will not despise. Accept these our first fruits, given in love, so that your Word may not return to you empty, and that in your church may truly dwell the fullness of Christ, who fills all in all.

The Blessing

May Jesus Christ, the beloved of God,
rule in your hearts and in your homes.
May the reign of God come to earth in glory and majesty,
with the Son seated at the right hand of power.
Amen! Come, Lord Jesus!

Index of Scripture Readings

TEXT	EVENT	PAGE
Genesis 1:1–2:4a	Trinity Sunday	153
Genesis 2:15–17; 3:1–7	First Sunday in Lent	76
Genesis 6:9–22; 7:24; 8:14–19	Proper 4—Ordinary Time 9	156
Genesis 12:1–4a	Second Sunday in Lent	79
Genesis 12:1–9	Proper 5—Ordinary Time 10	159
Genesis 18:1–15 (21:1–7)	Proper 6—Ordinary Time 11	162
Genesis 21:8–21	Proper 7—Ordinary Time 12	166
Genesis 22:1–14	Proper 8—Ordinary Time 13	169
Genesis 24:34–38, 42–49, 58–67	Proper 9—Ordinary Time 14	172
Genesis 25:19–34	Proper 10—Ordinary Time 15	176
Genesis 28:10–19a	Proper 11—Ordinary Time 16	179
Genesis 29:15–28	Proper 12—Ordinary Time 17	182
Genesis 32:22–31	Proper 13—Ordinary Time 18	186
Genesis 37:1–4, 12–28	Proper 14—Ordinary Time 19	189
Genesis 45:1–15	Proper 15—Ordinary Time 20	192
Exodus 1:8—2:10	Proper 16—Ordinary Time 21	195
Exodus 3:1–15	Proper 17—Ordinary Time 22	198
Exodus 12:1–14	Proper 18—Ordinary Time 23	201
Exodus 12:1–4 (5–10) 11–14	Maundy Thursday [ABC]	111
Exodus 14:19–31	Proper 19—Ordinary Time 24	204

Index of Scripture Readings

TEXT	EVENT	PAGE
Exodus 15:1b–11	Proper 19—Ordinary Time 24	204
Exodus 16:2–15	Proper 20—Ordinary Time 25	207
Exodus 17:1–7	Third Sunday in Lent	82
Exodus 17:1–7	Proper 21—Ordinary Time 26	210
Exodus 20:1–4, 7–9, 12–20	Proper 22—Ordinary Time 27	213
Exodus 24:12–18	Last Sunday After Epiphany (Transfiguration Sunday)	65
Exodus 32:1–14	Proper 23—Ordinary Time 28	216
Exodus 33:12–23	Proper 24—Ordinary Time 29	219
Leviticus 19:1–2, 9–18	Seventh Sunday After Epiphany / Proper 2—Ordinary Time 7	57
Numbers 11:24–30	Pentecost	147
Deuteronomy 30:15–20	Sixth Sunday After Epiphany / Proper 1—Ordinary Time 6	53
Deuteronomy 34:1–12	Proper 25—Ordinary Time 30	222
Joshua 3:7–17	Proper 26—Ordinary Time 31	225
Joshua 24:1–3a, 14–25	Proper 27—Ordinary Time 32	231
Judges 4:1–7	Proper 28—Ordinary Time 33	234
1 Samuel 16:1–13	Fourth Sunday in Lent	85
Psalm 2	Last Sunday After Epiphany (Transfiguration Sunday)	65
Psalm 8	Trinity Sunday	153
Psalm 13	Proper 8—Ordinary Time 13	169
Psalm 15	Fourth Sunday After Epiphany—Ordinary Time 4	46

Index of Scripture Readings

TEXT	EVENT	PAGE
Psalm 16	Second Sunday of Easter	124
Psalm 17:1–7, 15	Proper 13—Ordinary Time 18	186
Psalm 19	Proper 22—Ordinary Time 27	213
Psalm 22	Good Friday [ABC]	114
Psalm 23	Fourth Sunday in Lent	85
Psalm 23	Fourth Sunday of Easter	131
Psalm 27:1, 4–9	Third Sunday After Epiphany—Ordinary Time 3	43
Psalm 29	First Sunday After Epiphany—Ordinary Time 1	37
Psalm 31:1–5, 15–16	Fifth Sunday of Easter	134
Psalm 31:9–16	Sixth Sunday in Lent (Passion Sunday)	96
Psalm 32	First Sunday in Lent	76
Psalm 33:1–12	Proper 5—Ordinary Time 10	159
Psalm 34:1–10, 22	All Saint's Day / November 1	228
Psalm 36:5–11	Monday of Holy Week [ABC]	100
Psalm 40:1–11	Second Sunday After Epiphany—Ordinary Time 2	40
Psalm 45:10–17	Proper 9—Ordinary Time 14	172
Psalm 46	Proper 4—Ordinary Time 9	156
Psalm 47	Ascension of the Lord [ABC]	141
Psalm 51:1–17	Ash Wednesday [ABC]	71
Psalm 66:8–20	Sixth Sunday of Easter	137
Psalm 68:1–10, 32–35	Seventh Sunday of Easter	144
Psalm 70	Wednesday of Holy Week [ABC]	108
Psalm 71:1–14	Tuesday of Holy Week [ABC]	104
Psalm 72:1–7, 18–19	Second Sunday of Advent	7
Psalm 72:1–7, 10–14	Epiphany [ABC]	34
Psalm 78:1–7	Proper 27—Ordinary Time 32	231
Psalm 78:1–4, 12–16	Proper 21—Ordinary Time 26	210
Psalm 80:1–7, 17–19	Fourth Sunday of Advent	13
Psalm 86:1–10, 16–17	Proper 7—Ordinary Time 12	166
Psalm 90:1–6, 13–17	Proper 25—Ordinary Time 30	222

TEXT	EVENT	PAGE
Psalm 93	Ascension of the Lord [ABC]	141
Psalm 95	Third Sunday in Lent	82
Psalm 96	Christmas, First Proper [ABC] (Christmas Eve)	16
Psalm 97	Christmas, Second Proper [ABC] (Christmas Morning)	19
Psalm 98	Christmas, Third Proper [ABC] (Christmas Day)	23
Psalm 99	Last Sunday After Epiphany (Transfiguration Sunday)	65
Psalm 99	Proper 24—Ordinary Time 29	219
Psalm 100	Proper 29—Ordinary Time 34 (Christ the King or Reign of Christ)	237
Psalm 104:24-34, 35b	Pentecost	147
Psalm 105:1-11, 45b	Proper 12—Ordinary Time 17	182
Psalm 105:1-6, 16-22, 45b	Proper 14—Ordinary Time 19	189
Psalm 105:1-6, 23-26, 45c	Proper 17—Ordinary Time 22	198
Psalm 105:1-6, 37-45	Proper 20—Ordinary Time 25	207
Psalm 106:1-6, 19-23	Proper 23—Ordinary Time 28	216
Psalm 107:1-7, 33-37	Proper 26—Ordinary Time 31	225
Psalm 112:1-9 (10)	Fifth Sunday After Epiphany — Ordinary Time 5	49
Psalm 114	Easter Evening [ABC]	121
Psalm 114	Proper 19—Ordinary Time 24	204
Psalm 116:1-4, 12-19	Third Sunday of Easter	128
Psalm 116:1-2, 12-19	Proper 6—Ordinary Time 11	162
Psalm 116:1-2, 12-19	Maundy Thursday [ABC]	111
Psalm 118:1-2, 14-24	Easter (The Resurrection of the Lord)	118
Psalm 118:1-2, 19-29	Sixth Sunday in Lent (Palm Sunday)	92
Psalm 119:1-8	Sixth Sunday After Epiphany / Proper 1—Ordinary Time 6	53
Psalm 119:33-40	Seventh Sunday After Epiphany / Proper 2—Ordinary Time 7	57

Index of Scripture Readings

TEXT	EVENT	PAGE
Psalm 119:105–12	Proper 10—Ordinary Time 15	176
Psalm 121	Second Sunday in Lent	79
Psalm 122	First Sunday of Advent	3
Psalm 123	Proper 28—Ordinary Time 33	234
Psalm 124	Proper 16—Ordinary Time 21	195
Psalm 128	Proper 12—Ordinary Time 17	182
Psalm 130	Fifth Sunday in Lent	88
Psalm 131	Eighth Sunday After Epiphany / Proper 3—Ordinary Time 8	61
Psalm 133	Proper 15—Ordinary Time 20	192
Psalm 139:1–12, 23–24	Proper 11—Ordinary Time 16	179
Psalm 146:5–10	Third Sunday of Advent	10
Psalm 147:12–20	Second Sunday After Christmas [ABC]	31
Psalm 148	First Sunday After Christmas	27
Psalm 149	Proper 18—Ordinary Time 23	201
Song of Solomon 2:8–13	Proper 9—Ordinary Time 14	172
Isaiah 2:1–5	First Sunday of Advent	3
Isaiah 7:10–16	Fourth Sunday of Advent	13
Isaiah 9:1–4	Third Sunday After Epiphany—Ordinary Time 3	43
Isaiah 9:2–7	Christmas, First Proper [ABC] (Christmas Eve)	16
Isaiah 11:1–10	Second Sunday of Advent	7
Isaiah 25:6–9	Easter Evening [ABC]	121
Isaiah 35:1–10	Third Sunday of Advent	10
Isaiah 42:1–9	First Sunday After Epiphany—Ordinary Time 1	37
Isaiah 42:1–9	Monday of Holy Week [ABC]	100
Isaiah 49:1–7	Tuesday of Holy Week [ABC]	104
Isaiah 49:1–7	Second Sunday After Epiphany—Ordinary Time 2	40

Index of Scripture Readings

TEXT	EVENT	PAGE
Isaiah 49:8–16a	Eighth Sunday After Epiphany / Proper 3—Ordinary Time 8	61
Isaiah 50:4–9a	Sixth Sunday in Lent (Palm Sunday)	92
Isaiah 50:4–9a	Sixth Sunday in Lent (Passion Sunday)	96
Isaiah 50:4–9a	Wednesday of Holy Week [ABC]	108
Isaiah 52:7–10	Christmas, Third Proper [ABC] (Christmas Day)	23
Isaiah 52:12—53:12	Good Friday [ABC]	114
Isaiah 58:1–9a (9b–12)	Fifth Sunday After Epiphany — Ordinary Time 5	49
Isaiah 58:1–12	Ash Wednesday [ABC]	71
Isaiah 60:1–6	Epiphany [ABC]	34
Isaiah 62:6–12	Christmas, Second Proper [ABC] (Christmas Morning)	19
Isaiah 63:7–9	First Sunday After Christmas	27
Jeremiah 31:1–6	Easter (The Resurrection of the Lord)	118
Jeremiah 31:7–14	Second Sunday After Christmas [ABC]	31
Ezekiel 34:11–16, 20–24	Proper 29—Ordinary Time 34 (Christ the King or Reign of Christ)	237
Ezekiel 37:1–14	Fifth Sunday in Lent	88
Joel 2:1–2, 12–17	Ash Wednesday [ABC]	71
Micah 6:1–8	Fourth Sunday After Epiphany—Ordinary Time 4	46
Matthew 1:18–25	Fourth Sunday of Advent	13
Matthew 2:1–12	Epiphany [ABC]	34
Matthew 2:13–23	First Sunday After Christmas	27
Matthew 3:1–12	Second Sunday of Advent	7
Matthew 3:13–17	First Sunday After Epiphany—Ordinary Time 1	37

Index of Scripture Readings

TEXT	EVENT	PAGE
Matthew 4:1–11	First Sunday in Lent	76
Matthew 4:12–23	Third Sunday After Epiphany—Ordinary Time 3	43
Matthew 5:1–12	Fourth Sunday After Epiphany—Ordinary Time 4	46
Matthew 5:1–12	All Saint's Day / November 1	228
Matthew 5:13–20	Fifth Sunday After Epiphany — Ordinary Time 5	49
Matthew 5:21–37	Sixth Sunday After Epiphany / Proper 1—Ordinary Time 6	53
Matthew 5:38–48	Seventh Sunday After Epiphany / Proper 2—Ordinary Time 7	57
Matthew 6:1–6, 16–21	Ash Wednesday [ABC]	71
Matthew 6:24–34	Eighth Sunday After Epiphany / Proper 3—Ordinary Time 8	61
Matthew 7:21–29	Proper 4—Ordinary Time 9	156
Matthew 9:9–13, 18–26	Proper 5—Ordinary Time 10	159
Matthew 9:35—10:8 (9–23)	Proper 6—Ordinary Time 11	162
Matthew 10:24–39	Proper 7—Ordinary Time 12	166
Matthew 10:40–42	Proper 8—Ordinary Time 13	169
Matthew 11:2–11	Third Sunday of Advent	10
Matthew 11:16–19, 25–30	Proper 9—Ordinary Time 14	172
Matthew 13:1–9, 18–23	Proper 10—Ordinary Time 15	176
Matthew 13:24–30, 36–43	Proper 11—Ordinary Time 16	179
Matthew 13:31–33, 44–52	Proper 12—Ordinary Time 17	182
Matthew 14:13–21	Proper 13—Ordinary Time 18	186
Matthew 14:22–33	Proper 14—Ordinary Time 19	189
Matthew 15:(10–20) 21–28	Proper 15—Ordinary Time 20	192
Matthew 16:13–20	Proper 16—Ordinary Time 21	195
Matthew 16:21–28	Proper 17—Ordinary Time 22	198
Matthew 17:1–9	Last Sunday After Epiphany (Transfiguration Sunday)	65
Matthew 18:15–20	Proper 18—Ordinary Time 23	201

Index of Scripture Readings

TEXT	EVENT	PAGE
Matthew 18:21–35	Proper 19—Ordinary Time 24	204
Matthew 20:1–16	Proper 20—Ordinary Time 25	207
Matthew 21:1–11	Sixth Sunday in Lent (Palm Sunday)	92
Matthew 21:23–32	Proper 21—Ordinary Time 26	210
Matthew 21:33–46	Proper 22—Ordinary Time 27	213
Matthew 22:1–14	Proper 23—Ordinary Time 28	216
Matthew 22:15–22	Proper 24—Ordinary Time 29	219
Matthew 22:34–46	Proper 25—Ordinary Time 30	222
Matthew 23:1–12	Proper 26—Ordinary Time 31	225
Matthew 24:36–44	First Sunday of Advent	3
Matthew 25:1–13	Proper 27—Ordinary Time 32	231
Matthew 25:14–30	Proper 28—Ordinary Time 33	234
Matthew 25:31–46	Proper 29—Ordinary Time 34 (Christ the King or Reign of Christ)	237
Matthew 26:14—27:66	Sixth Sunday in Lent (Passion Sunday)	96
Matthew 27:11–54	Sixth Sunday in Lent (Passion Sunday)	96
Matthew 28:1–10	Easter (The Resurrection of the Lord)	118
Matthew 28:16–20	Trinity Sunday	153
Luke 1:47–55	Third Sunday of Advent	10
Luke 2:1–14 (15–20)	Christmas, First Proper [ABC] (Christmas Eve)	16
Luke 2:(1–7) 8–20	Christmas, Second Proper [ABC] (Christmas Morning)	19
Luke 24:13–35	Third Sunday of Easter	128
Luke 24:13–49	Easter Evening [ABC]	121
Luke 24:44–53	Ascension of the Lord [ABC]	141
John 1:1–14	Christmas, Third Proper [ABC] (Christmas Day)	23
John 1:(1–9) 10–18	Second Sunday After Christmas [ABC]	31
John 1:29–42	Second Sunday After Epiphany—Ordinary Time 2	40
John 3:1–17	Second Sunday in Lent	79

Index of Scripture Readings 249

TEXT	EVENT	PAGE
John 4:5–42	Third Sunday in Lent	82
John 7:37–39	Pentecost	147
John 9:1–41	Fourth Sunday in Lent	85
John 10:1–10	Fourth Sunday of Easter	131
John 11:1–45	Fifth Sunday in Lent	88
John 12:1–11	Monday of Holy Week [ABC]	100
John 12:20–36	Tuesday of Holy Week [ABC]	104
John 13:1–17, 31b–35	Maundy Thursday [ABC]	111
John 13:21–32	Wednesday of Holy Week [ABC]	108
John 14:1–14	Fifth Sunday of Easter	134
John 14:15–21	Sixth Sunday of Easter	137
John 17:1–11	Seventh Sunday of Easter	144
John 18:1—19:42	Good Friday [ABC]	114
John 20:1–18	Easter (The Resurrection of the Lord)	118
John 20:19–23	Pentecost	147
John 20:19–31	Second Sunday of Easter	124
Acts 1:1–11	Ascension of the Lord [ABC]	141
Acts 1:6–14	Seventh Sunday of Easter	144
Acts 2:1–21	Pentecost	147
Acts 2:14a, 22–32	Second Sunday of Easter	124
Acts 2:14a, 36–41	Third Sunday of Easter	128
Acts 2:42–47	Fourth Sunday of Easter	131
Acts 7:55–60	Fifth Sunday of Easter	134
Acts 10:34–43	First Sunday After Epiphany—Ordinary Time 1	37
Acts 10:34–43	Easter (The Resurrection of the Lord)	118
Acts 17:22–31	Sixth Sunday of Easter	137
Romans 1:1–7	Fourth Sunday of Advent	13
Romans 1:16–17; 3:22b–28 (29–31)	Proper 4—Ordinary Time 9	156
Romans 4:1–5, 13–17	Second Sunday in Lent	79

TEXT	EVENT	PAGE
Romans 4:13–25	Proper 5—Ordinary Time 10	159
Romans 5:1–8	Proper 6—Ordinary Time 11	162
Romans 5:1–11	Third Sunday in Lent	82
Romans 5:12–19	First Sunday in Lent	76
Romans 6:1b–11	Proper 7—Ordinary Time 12	166
Romans 6:12–23	Proper 8—Ordinary Time 13	169
Romans 7:15–25a	Proper 9—Ordinary Time 14	172
Romans 8:1–11	Proper 10—Ordinary Time 15	176
Romans 8:6–11	Fifth Sunday in Lent	88
Romans 8:12–25	Proper 11—Ordinary Time 16	179
Romans 8:26–39	Proper 12—Ordinary Time 17	182
Romans 9:1–5	Proper 13—Ordinary Time 18	186
Romans 10:5–15	Proper 14—Ordinary Time 19	189
Romans 11:1–2a, 29–32	Proper 15—Ordinary Time 20	192
Romans 12:1–8	Proper 16—Ordinary Time 21	195
Romans 12:9–21	Proper 17—Ordinary Time 22	198
Romans 13:8–14	Proper 18—Ordinary Time 23	201
Romans 13:11–14	First Sunday of Advent	3
Romans 14:1–12	Proper 19—Ordinary Time 24	204
Romans 15:4–13	Second Sunday of Advent	7
1 Corinthians 1:1–9	Second Sunday After Epiphany—Ordinary Time 2	40
1 Corinthians 1:10–18	Third Sunday After Epiphany—Ordinary Time 3	43
1 Corinthians 1:18–31	Fourth Sunday After Epiphany—Ordinary Time 4	46
1 Corinthians 1:18–31	Tuesday of Holy Week [ABC]	104
1 Corinthians 2:1–12 (13–16)	Fifth Sunday After Epiphany — Ordinary Time 5	49
1 Corinthians 3:1–9	Sixth Sunday After Epiphany / Proper 1—Ordinary Time 6	53
1 Corinthians 3:10–11, 16–23	Seventh Sunday After Epiphany / Proper 2—Ordinary Time 7	57

Index of Scripture Readings

TEXT	EVENT	PAGE
1 Corinthians 4:1–5	Eighth Sunday After Epiphany / Proper 3—Ordinary Time 8	61
1 Corinthians 5:6b–8	Easter Evening [ABC]	121
1 Corinthians 11:23–26	Maundy Thursday [ABC]	111
1 Corinthians 12:3b–13	Pentecost	147
2 Corinthians 5:20b—6:10	Ash Wednesday [ABC]	71
2 Corinthians 13:11–13	Trinity Sunday	153
Ephesians 1:3–14	Second Sunday After Christmas [ABC]	31
Ephesians 1:15–23	Ascension of the Lord [ABC]	141
Ephesians 1:15–23	Proper 29—Ordinary Time 34 (Christ the King or Reign of Christ)	237
Ephesians 3:1–12	Epiphany [ABC]	34
Ephesians 5:8–14	Fourth Sunday in Lent	85
Philippians 1:21–30	Proper 20—Ordinary Time 25	207
Philippians 2:1–13	Proper 21—Ordinary Time 26	210
Philippians 2:5–11	Sixth Sunday in Lent (Palm Sunday)	92
Philippians 2:5–11	Sixth Sunday in Lent (Passion Sunday)	96
Philippians 3:4b–14	Proper 22—Ordinary Time 27	213
Philippians 4:1–9	Proper 23—Ordinary Time 28	216
Colossians 3:1–4	Easter (The Resurrection of the Lord)	118
1 Thessalonians 1:1–10	Proper 24—Ordinary Time 29	219
1 Thessalonians 2:1–8	Proper 25—Ordinary Time 30	222
1 Thessalonians 2:9–13	Proper 26—Ordinary Time 31	225
1 Thessalonians 4:13–18	Proper 27—Ordinary Time 32	231
1 Thessalonians 5:1–11	Proper 28—Ordinary Time 33	234

Index of Scripture Readings

TEXT	EVENT	PAGE
Titus 2:11–14	Christmas, First Proper [ABC] (Christmas Eve)	16
Titus 3:4–7	Christmas, Second Proper [ABC] (Christmas Morning)	19
Hebrews 1:1–4 (5–12)	Christmas, Third Proper [ABC] (Christmas Day)	23
Hebrews 2:10–18	First Sunday After Christmas	27
Hebrews 4:14–16; 5:7–9	Good Friday [ABC]	114
Hebrews 9:11–15	Monday of Holy Week [ABC]	100
Hebrews 12:1–3	Wednesday of Holy Week [ABC]	108
Hebrews 10:16–25	Good Friday [ABC]	114
James 5:7–10	Third Sunday of Advent	10
1 Peter 1:3–9	Second Sunday of Easter	124
1 Peter 1:17–23	Third Sunday of Easter	128
1 Peter 2:19–25	Fourth Sunday of Easter	131
1 Peter 2:2–10	Fifth Sunday of Easter	134
1 Peter 3:13–22	Sixth Sunday of Easter	137
1 Peter 4:12–14; 5:6–11	Seventh Sunday of Easter	144
2 Peter 1:16–21	Last Sunday After Epiphany (Transfiguration Sunday)	65
1 John 3:1–3	All Saint's Day / November 1	228
Revelation 7:9–17	All Saint's Day / November 1	228

www.ingramcontent.com/pod-product-compliance
Lightning Source LLC
Chambersburg PA
CBHW030613230426
43661CB00053B/1960